A Book of Days

Wisdom Through the Seasons

Edited by

Elizabeth Pepper and John Wilcock

CAPRA PRESS
SANTA BARBARA

*To those who enjoy
company along the way.*

LIBRARY OF CONGRESS CATALOGING-IN-PUBLICATION DATA
A book of days : wisdom through the seasons / edited by
Elizabeth Pepper and John Wilcock.
p.   cm.
ISBN 0-88496-406-X (pbk.)
1. Life—Quotations, maxims, etc. 2. Conduct of life—Quotations, maxims, etc.
I. Pepper, Elizabeth. II. Wilcock, John.
PN6084.L53B66   1996
808.8'2—dc20   96-5311
                                                                   CIP

CAPRA PRESS
P.O. Box 2068, Santa Barbara, CA 93120

FOREWORD

FOR CENTURIES humans have pondered the wonder and the pain of life on Earth with the very experience of being alive producing its own treasury of collected wisdom. From this rich source we have selected a wide range of thoughts, all of them dealing with life's reality and illusion. Inspired by the style and purpose of the medieval Books of Days, we match our chosen words to the pattern and passage of time.

A single year may represent a lifetime, for each can be divided into four seasons. Spring belongs to youth and renewal; summer's gifts are maturity and fruitfulness; autumn reaps the harvest and winter brings rest and regeneration. This natural cycle of seasons keynotes the harmony of every living thing and to sense the underlying themes, their form and cadence, is to begin to understand the quality of life's mystery.

Be ready to accept guidance from earlier sages, from the voices of those who have traveled this way before, as they offer comfort and advice in words of wit and beauty, clarity and common sense.

Now, in the words of Horace, the Roman poet who flourished during the first century B.C.: *Dare to be wise. Begin!*

Spring

MARCH

Come, fill the Cup, and in the fire of Spring
The Winter-garment of Repentance fling;
The Bird of Time has but a little way
To fly — and Lo! the Bird is on the Wing.

—OMAR KHAYYAM

THE MONTH of March, from the Latin *Martius* or Mars, is named for the Roman god of war but long before Greek culture dominated Rome, Mars was a simple rural deity concerned with the earth and its bounty. His function as guardian of crops and farm animals caused his subsequent identification with the fierce and ruthless Ares. The Roman concept of the warrior-god differed from the Greek, being more inclined to defense than offense.

The fifteenth-century woodcut illustrates March activities as fishing and pruning the grape arbor: passive labor in Pisces and lively work under the sign of Aries. Pisces, depicted with three fishes rather than with the conventional two, occupies the first three weeks of the month, a watery time of change during which winter's ice melts away and the earth softens. The sun's return to the northern hemisphere is markedly evident at the vernal equinox when day and night are of equal length; spring arrives with the fiery Ram of Aries.

Hope and dream, wish and imagine as the human spirit probes the mystery of being on earth. Fish for reasons, prune to let in plenty of light and till the soil to uncover its secret potential. This is our beginning.

All is one.

—GREEK PROVERB

All things are in motion.
  Nothing steadfastly is.

—ARISTOTLE

Nothing ever is,
  everything is becoming.

—PLATO

The sum of things is
  unlimited, and they all
  change into one another.

—LEUCIPPUS

It takes a certain amount
  of intelligence and imagination to
  realize the extraordinary queerness
  and mysteriousness of the world
  in which we live.

—ALDOUS HUXLEY

The universe may be not only
  queerer than we suppose,
  but queerer than we can suppose.

—JOHN SCOTT HALDANE

We and the cosmos are one.
  The cosmos is a vast living body,
  of which we are still parts.

—D. H. LAWRENCE

No doubt the spirit and energy
  of the world is what is acting in us,
  as the sea is what rises in every
  little wave; but it passes through us;
  and cry out as we may, it will
  move on. Our privilege is
  to have perceived it as it moved.

—GEORGE SANTAYANA

The universe is full of magical things
  patiently waiting for our wits
  to grow sharper.

—EDEN PHILLPOTTS

Let us not look back in anger
  or forward in fear, but around
  in awareness.

—JAMES THURBER

The ultimate value of life
  depends upon awareness, and
  the power of contemplation
  rather than upon mere survival.

—ARISTOTLE

The first principles of the universe are
  atoms and empty space; everything
  else is merely thought to exist.

—DEMOCRITUS

The universe is change; our life is
  what our thoughts make it.

—MARCUS AURELIUS

Thinking is identical with being.

—PARMENIDES

The great object of life
is sensation — to feel that we exist,
even though in pain.

—LORD BYRON

Nothing ever becomes real till
it is experienced — even a proverb
is no proverb to you till your life
has illustrated it.

—JOHN KEATS

Life is the art of drawing
sufficient conclusions from
insufficient premises.

—SAMUEL BUTLER

The very meaninglessness of life
forces a man to create his own
meaning.

—STANLEY KUBRICK

I have in my own fashion learned
the lesson that life is effort,
unremittingly repeated.

—HENRY JAMES

The world is nothing but
an endless seesaw.

—MONTAIGNE

The universe is not hostile, nor yet is
it friendly. It is simply indifferent.

—JOHN HAYNES HOLMES

This is a lesson we cannot
learn too soon, that the world
can go on easily without us.

—GOETHE

There are three gates of perception
upon the universe: the sensual,
the intellectual, and the emotional.

—BLAISE PASCAL

If the doors of perception were
cleansed, everything would appear
to man as it is, infinite.

—WILLIAM BLAKE

I don't believe life has a purpose. Life
is a lot of protoplasm with an urge to
reproduce and continue in being.

—JOSEPH CAMPBELL

The absurd is the essential concept
and the first truth.

—ALBERT CAMUS

Apart from man, no being
wonders at its own existence.

—SCHOPENHAUER

Who knows but that man's reason for
existence may be his existence itself.

—JULIEN OFFRAY DE LA METTRIE

The art of life lies in a constant
readjustment to our surroundings.

—OKAKURA KAKUZO

The first great rule of life
is to put up with things.

—BALTASAR GRACIAN

As I grow to understand life less and
less, I learn to live it more and more.

—JULES RENARD

Life is the gift of nature; beautiful
living is the gift of wisdom.

—CELTIC ADAGE

Adopt the pace of nature;
her secret is patience.

—EMERSON

In nature there are neither rewards
nor punishments — there are
consequences.

—ROBERT G. INGERSOLL

If one way be better than another,
that you may be sure is nature's way.

—ARISTOTLE

We cannot fail in following nature.

—MONTAIGNE

The end is living
in agreement with nature.

—ZENO

Man is the measure of all things.

—PROTAGORAS

Only a man who masters himself
can gain freedom from the forces
which govern all things.

—GOETHE

Self-control is the quality that
distinguishes the fittest to survive.

—GEORGE BERNARD SHAW

Favor and disgrace cause one dismay;
what we value and what we fear
are within our self.

—LAO-TSE

We are born, so to speak, in a
temporary form somewhere,
and then, bit by bit, we create
our birthplaces within us, in order
to be reborn there each day,
in a more definitive way.

—RILKE

Learn to limit yourself, to content
yourself with some definite thing
and some definite work; dare
to be what you are, and learn to
resign with a good grace all
that you are not, and to believe in
your own individuality.

—HENRI FRÉDÉRIC AMIEL

Be content to seem
what you really are.

—MARTIAL

The only thing worth the trouble
in this life is oneself.

—STENDHAL

There is only one of you in all of time.

—MARTHA GRAHAM

Know thyself.

—GREEK PROVERB

The most difficult thing in life
is knowledge of yourself.

—THALES

It is as hard to see one's self as to look
backwards without turning around.

—THOREAU

What is the self? I haven't the
slightest idea. I awoke one day on
this earth; I found myself bound
to a body, a character, a fate. Shall I
amuse myself vainly seeking to
change them while forgetting
in the process to live?

—STENDHAL

Reverence yourself.

—PYTHAGORAS

A man who finds no satisfaction
in himself, seeks for it in vain
elsewhere.

—LA ROCHEFOUCAULD

To know oneself is a matter of
great importance in the world,
so also it is important to be able
to estimate the strength of one's
mental and physical powers.

—MACHIAVELLI

Men only take their needs into
consideration — never their abilities.

—NAPOLEON I

Sometimes it is more important
to discover what one cannot do,
than what one can do.

—LIN YUTANG

Who has self-confidence
will lead the rest.

—HORACE

"Know thyself" is indeed a weighty
admonition. But in this, as in any
science, the difficulties are discovered
only by those who set their hands
to it. We must push against a door to
find out whether it is bolted or not.

—MONTAIGNE

The first and simplest emotion
which we discover in the
human mind is curiosity.

—EDMUND BURKE

What is wanted is not the
will-to-believe, but the wish to
find out, which is its exact opposite.

—BERTRAND RUSSELL

The will of a sound mind
is the desire of a possible thing.

—REGINALD SCOT

The great business of a man is
to improve his mind: all other
projects and pursuits, whether
in our power to compass or not,
are only amusements.

—PLINY THE ELDER

A good mind is lord of a kingdom.

—SENECA

All that we are is the result
of what we have thought.

—BUDDHA

If there is no other attribute which
belongs to man as man except reason,
then reason will be his one good,
worth all the rest put together.

—SENECA

To live is to think.

—CICERO

I will stop at no point as long as
  clear reasoning will carry me further.

—THOMAS HENRY HUXLEY

I see but one rule: to be clear.
  If I am not clear, all my world
  crumbles to nothing.

—STENDHAL

What can I know?
  What ought I to do?
  What may I hope?

—IMMANUEL KANT

The greatest security in this
  tumultuous world is faith
  in your own mind.

—SUSANNE LANGER

Every life is a profession of faith,
  and exercises an inevitable
  and silent influence.

—HENRI FRÉDÉRIC AMIEL

Faith consists in believing
  when it is beyond the
  power of reason to believe.

—VOLTAIRE

You can do very little with faith,
  but you can do nothing without it.

—SAMUEL BUTLER

If there is a faith that can
  move mountains, it is faith
  in your own power.

—MARIE VON EBNER-ESCHENBACH

I think it is impossible to explain faith.
It is like trying to explain air, which
one cannot do by dividing it into its
component parts and labeling them
scientifically. It must be breathed
to be understood.

—PATRICK WHITE

To live at all is a kind of rashness,
  but it is better to live than not to live.

—ERASMUS

Life only demands from you
  the strength that you possess.
  Only one feat is possible — not
  to have run away.

—DAG HAMMARSKJÖLD

Nothing in life is to be feared;
  it is only to be understood.

—MARIE CURIE

Be not afraid of life. Believe that
  life is worth living, and your belief
  will help create the fact.

—WILLIAM JAMES

Not all those who know their minds
  know their heart as well.

        —LA ROCHEFOUCAULD

What the heart knows today,
  the head understands tomorrow.

        —IRISH PROVERB

In vain we fly from what
  we bear in our heart.

        —MME. DE SÉVIGNÉ

Everything we love, no doubt,
  will pass away, perhaps tomorrow,
  perhaps thousands of years later.
  Neither it nor our love for it is any
  the less valuable for that reason.

        —JOHN PASSMORE

It is the heart that makes the man,
  all the rest is rubbish.

        —PETRONIUS ARBITER

It is his own heart and not the
  opinion of others that honor a man.

        —SCHILLER

It is only with the heart
  that one can see rightly; what
  is essential is invisible to the eye.

        —ANTOINE DE SAINT-EXUPÉRY

Great thoughts proceed
  from the heart.

        —VAUVENARGUES

It is wisdom to believe the heart.

        —GEORGE SANTAYANA

If you follow your bliss, you put
  yourself on a kind of track that has
  been there the whole while, waiting
  for you, and the life you ought to
  be living is the one you are living.

        —JOSEPH CAMPBELL

Our life is a tissue woven of wind.

—JOSEPH JOUBERT

The most difficult thing in life
is knowledge of yourself.

—THALES

Beware lest you lose the substance
by grasping at the shadow.

—AESOP

Abundance of knowledge
does not teach a man to be wise.

—HERACLITUS

All that we see or seem
is but a dream within a dream.

—EDGAR ALLAN POE

To know all things is not permitted.

—HORACE

Ignorance lies at the bottom
of all human knowledge,
and the deeper we penetrate
the nearer we arrive unto it.

—CHARLES CALEB COLTON

All that we know is nothing
can be known.

—SOCRATES

Freedom from the desire
for an answer is essential to the
understanding of a problem.

—KRISHNAMURTI

The most beautiful thing
we can experience is the mysterious.
It is the fundamental emotion
which stands at the cradle of
true art and true science.

—ALBERT EINSTEIN

I am entirely on the side of mystery.
I mean, any attempts to explain away
the mystery is ridiculous. I believe
in the profound and unfathomable
mystery of life which has a sort
of divine quality about it.

—ALDOUS HUXLEY

From magic we come, to magic we go.

—FRANK O'CONNOR

Where is your self to be found?
Always in the deepest enchantment
that you have experienced.

—HUGO VON HOFMANNSTHAL

The spirit is the true self.

—CICERO

I believe very deeply in the
human spirit, and I have
a sense of awe about it.

—HORTON FOOTE

The people I respect must behave as if
they were immortal and as if society
were eternal. Both assumptions
are false; both of them must be
accepted as true if we are to go on
working and eating and loving,
and are to keep open a few breathing
holes for the human spirit.

—E. M. FORSTER

It better befits a man to laugh at life
than to lament over it.

—SENECA

Not a shred of evidence exists in favor
of the idea that life is serious.

—BRENDAN GILL

Look everywhere with your eyes;
but with your soul never look
at many things, but at one.

—V. V. ROZANOV

The soul of man is divided into
three parts: intelligence and passion
are possessed by other animals as
well, but reason by man alone.
The soul is distinct from life;
it is immortal, since that from
which it is detached is immortal.
Reason is immortal, all else mortal.

—PYTHAGORAS

The soul is identical with reason.

—DEMOCRITUS

Every man who refuses to accept
the conditions of life sells his soul.

—CHARLES BAUDELAIRE

The body is a thing, the soul is also
a thing; man is not a thing, but
a drama — his life. Man has to live
with the body and soul which have
fallen to him by chance. And
the first thing he has to do is
decide what he is going to do.

—ORTEGA Y GASSET

Man's character is his fate.

—HERACLITUS

Behavior is a mirror in which everyone
displays his own image.

—GOETHE

In goodness there are
all kinds of wisdom.

—EURIPIDES

Hold faithfulness and sincerity
as first principles.

—CONFUCIUS

On the mountains of truth
you never climb in vain.

—NIETZSCHE

All the animals except man know
that the principle business of life
is to enjoy it.

—SAMUEL BUTLER

Pythagoras used to say life resembles
the Olympic Games: a few men strain
their muscles to carry off a prize;
others bring trinkets to sell to the
crowd for gain; and some there are,
and not the worst, who seek no other
profit than to look at the show
and see how and why everything
is done; spectators of the life
of other men in order to judge
and regulate their own.

—MONTAIGNE

The secret of happiness is curiosity.

—NORMAN DOUGLAS

Knowledge of what is possible
is the beginning of happiness.

—LUCRETIUS

One's happiness must in some measure
be always at the mercy of chance.

—JANE AUSTEN

Happiness is not steadfast
but transient.

—EURIPIDES

Happiness in this world, when it
comes, comes incidentally. Make it
an object of pursuit, and it leads us
a wild-goose chase, and is never
attained. Follow some other object,
and very possibly we may find
that we have caught happiness
without dreaming of it.

—NATHANIEL HAWTHORNE

The world as an object of experience
would be no less picturesque
for having a simple explanation.

—GEORGE SANTAYANA

By means of the easy and the
simple we grasp the laws of the
whole world. When the laws of
the whole world are grasped,
therein lies perfection.

—THE I CHING

Life is a privilege and a challenge.
Endeavor to be as perfect as you can.

—SAMUEL JOHNSON

Spring

APRIL

Happy the man, and happy he alone,
He, who can call today his own:
He who, secure within, can say,
Tomorrow do thy worst, for I have lived today.

—JOHN DRYDEN

PRIL, the delight of poets, has its own singular quality. Expectancy, the thrill of anticipation, is born with the advent of spring. April's very name, it is said, stems from the Latin word *aperire* meaning "to open". Trees and plants come to bud, migrating birds fill the air with song, soft rains and gentle winds promise the joy of renewal — a splendid opening indeed. Small wonder that the ancients welcomed the sun's return with feasting and pageantry.

Our medieval artist chose to illustrate the month of April with the figure of a young swain in fine apparel. With love on his mind, he carries a leafy bough in one hand, a floral tribute in the other. Behind him in a meadow sits the object of his affections who whiles away the time weaving a basket to hold treasures the future may bring.

The forceful Ram dominates most of April. The final week finds Taurus, the Bull, in charge — tempering urgency with down-to-earth practicality. April is the time to take action, sow seeds, set out on a journey. But allow care as well as daring to be your companion.

You must imagine your life,
and then it happens.

—JOHN UPDIKE

First, say to yourself what you would
be; and then do what you have to do.

—EPICTETUS

To become what we are capable of
becoming is the only end in life.

—ROBERT LOUIS STEVENSON

If one advances confidently in the
direction of his dreams, and
endeavors to live the life which he
has imagined, he will meet with a
success unexpected in common hours.

— THOREAU

The aim, if reached or not,
makes great the life: try to be
Shakespeare, leave the rest to fate.

—ROBERT BROWNING

No bird soars too high
if he soars with his own wings.

—WILLIAM BLAKE

There is always room at the top.

—DANIEL WEBSTER

The actual is limited,
the possible immense.

—LAMARTINE

Things sometimes become possible
if we want them enough

—T. S. ELIOT

To accomplish great things,
we must not only act, but also dream,
not only plan but also believe.

—ANATOLE FRANCE

Our life is composed greatly
from dreams, from the unconscious,
and they must be brought
into connection with action.
They must be woven together.

—ANAÏS NIN

The principle thing is not to remain
with the dream, with the intention,
with the being-in-the-mood,
but always forcibly to convert it
into all things.

—RILKE

Our bodies are our gardens, to which
our wills are gardeners.

—SHAKESPEARE

In life as in art perhaps our salvation
is the handful of seed out of which
we imagine gardens.

—WINFIELD T. SCOTT

To sow is less difficult than to reap.

—GOETHE

The seed dies into a new life,
and so does man.

—GEORGE MACDONALD

The courage to be as oneself
is the courage to make of oneself
what one wants to be.

—PAUL TILLICH

Chiefly the mould of a man's fortune
is in his own hands.

—SIR FRANCIS BACON

If you would create something,
you must be something.

—GOETHE

You cannot dream yourself into
a character; you must hammer
and forge one for yourself.

—JAMES E. FROUDE

If you can command yourself,
you can command the world.

—CHINESE PROVERB

The will of a man is his happiness.

—SCHILLER

Nothing is impossible to the man
who can will, and then do;
this is the only law of success.

—MIRABEAU

Success is the child of audacity.

—DISRAELI

Audacity augments courage;
hesitation fear.

—PUBLILIUS SYRUS

Courage is a kind of salvation.

—PLATO

Who dares nothing,
  need hope for nothing.

—SCHILLER

A bold attack is half the battle.

—GERMAN PROVERB

Fortune favors the brave.

—TERENCE

To think and feel we are able,
  is often to be so.

—JOEL HAWES

They conquer who believe they can.

—VIRGIL

Our doubts are traitors, and make us
  lose the good we oft might win by
  fearing to attempt.

—SHAKESPEARE

Believe you have it, and you have it.

—LATIN PROVERB

The bravest thing you can do
  when you are not brave is to
  profess courage and act accordingly.

—CORRA HARRIS

We know what we are,
  but know not what we may be.

—SHAKESPEARE

One does not know, cannot know,
  the best that is in one.

—NIETZSCHE

Only the bold get to the top.

—PUBLILIUS SYRUS

The surest way not to fail
is to determine to succeed.

—RICHARD BRINSLEY SHERIDAN

One should be booted and spurred
and ready to depart.

—MONTAIGNE

Chance is always powerful.
Let your hook be always cast;
in the pool where you least expect it,
there will be a fish.

—OVID

The wise and bold man is often
the architect of his own fortune.

—TASSO

A wise man will make
more opportunities than he finds.

—SIR FRANCIS BACON

Our deeds determine us,
as much as we determine our deeds.

—GEORGE ELIOT

Begin not with a program,
but with a deed.

—FLORENCE NIGHTINGALE

I ought, therefore I can.

—IMMANUEL KANT

Life can only be understood
backwards, but it
must be lived forwards.

—KIERKEGAARD

Don't let life discourage you;
everyone who got where he is
had to begin where he was.

—RICHARD L. EVANS

A good beginning
is half the battle.

—PORTUGUESE PROVERB

He that is over-cautious
will accomplish little.

—SCHILLER

Heaven never helps
the man who will not act.

—SOPHOCLES

Actions are the real substance of life;
words are merely its adornment.

—BALTASAR GRACIAN

Failures always overtake
those that have the power to do,
without the will to act.

—JAMES ELLIS

Let him that would move the world
first move himself.

—SOCRATES

Happiness springs from action.

—ARISTOTLE

Action makes more fortunes
than caution.

—VAUVENARGUES

Who has begun has half done.

—HORACE

Even if you're on the right
track, you'll get run over
if you just sit there.

—WILL ROGERS

The cure for grief is motion;
the recipe for strength is action.

—ELBERT G. HUBBARD

What does not destroy me,
makes me stronger.

—NIETZSCHE

Slight not what's near
by aiming at what's far.

—EURIPIDES

Even if it doesn't work, there
is something healthy and
invigorating about direct action.

—HENRY MILLER

Arouse yourself, gird your loins,
put aside idleness, grasp the nettle,
and do some hard work.

— ST. BERNARD OF CLAIRVAUX

The race is not to him
who runs the fastest,
but to him who starts soonest.

—RABELAIS

Get good counsel before
you begin; and when you
have decided, act promptly.

—SALLUST

Not everything should be speculation;
you must also act.

—BALTASAR GRACIAN

Procrastination is the art
of keeping up with yesterday.

—DON MARQUIS

Deliberate with caution,
but act with decision.

—CHARLES CALEB COLTON

Up sluggard, and waste not life;
in the grave will be sleeping enough.

—BENJAMIN FRANKLIN

There is no wealth but life.

—JOHN RUSKIN

Make use of time
for it flies away so fast.

—GOETHE

The man who procrastinates is
always struggling with misfortunes.

—HESIOD

Running is of no use;
the thing is to start in time.

—LA FONTAINE

Active natures are rarely
melancholy. Activity and
sadness are incompatible.

—CHRISTIAN NESTELL BOVEE

The happiness of man consists in life,
and life is in labor.

—TOLSTOY

Without labor nothing prospers.

—SOPHOCLES

The vices of idleness must
be shaken off with occupation.

—SENECA

Idleness is the enemy of the soul.

—ST. BENEDICT

It's not death that a man
should fear, but he should fear
never beginning to live.

—MARCUS AURELIUS

No man or a woman born, coward
or brave, can shun his destiny.

—HOMER

Purpose is what gives life a meaning.

—CHARLES H. PARKHURST

Have a purpose in life, and
having it, throw into your work
such strength of mind and muscle
as God has given you.

—THOMAS CARLYLE

There is a tide in the affairs of men,
which taken at the flood,
leads on to fortune; omitted,
all the voyage of their life is bound
in shallows and in miseries.

—SHAKESPEARE

Procrastination is the thief of time.

—EDWARD YOUNG

Seize the present day, trusting
the morrow as little as you can.

—HORACE

Only put off until tomorrow
what you are willing to die
having left undone.

—PABLO PICASSO

Waste of time is the most extravagant
and costly of all expenses.

—THEOPHRASTUS

We must take the current
when it serves, or lose our ventures.

—SHAKESPEARE

The secret of success
is constancy of purpose.

—DISRAELI

The way to be nothing
is to do nothing.

—NATHANIEL HOWE

Idleness is many gathered
miseries in one name.

—JEAN PAUL RICHTER

The busy man is troubled
with but one devil,
the idle man by a thousand.

—SPANISH PROVERB

I know only one truth.
Work alone creates happiness.
I am sure only of that thing,
and I forget it all the time.

—JULES RENARD

Blessed is he who has found his work.
Let him ask no other blessedness.

—THOMAS CARLYLE

The only way I keep afloat
is by working.

—VIRGINIA WOOLF

One is never drained by work but
only by idleness. Lack of work is the
most enervating thing in the world.

—JOHN STEINBECK

There is not a moment
without some duty.

—CICERO

Do the duty which lieth
nearest to thee ! Thy second duty
will already have become clearer.

—THOMAS CARLYLE

Whatever is worth doing at all,
is worth doing well.

—LORD CHESTERFIELD

The reward of a thing well done,
is to have done it.

—EMERSON

Exactness in little duties is a
wonderful source of cheerfulness.

—FREDERICK W. FABER

Every duty we omit, obscures some
truth which we should have known.

—JOHN RUSKIN

Who escapes a duty, avoids a gain.

—THEODORE PARKER

Things done well and with a care
exempt themselves from fear.

—SHAKESPEARE

Rest satisfied with doing well
and leave others to talk of you
as they please.

—PYTHAGORAS

The talent of success is nothing more
than doing what you can do well,
and doing well whatever you do,
without a thought of fame.

—LONGFELLOW

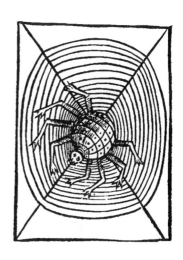

Quality is never a accident. It is always
the result of intelligent effort.

—JOHN RUSKIN

There is no failure
except in no longer trying.

—ELBERT G. HUBBARD

Experience shows that success
is due less to ability than to zeal.

—CHARLES BUXTON

All things are difficult
before they are easy.

—THOMAS FULLER

Whatever is worthwhile is difficult.

—OVID

No one knows until he tries.

—PUBLILIUS SYRUS

Difficulties strengthen the mind
as labor does the body.

—SENECA

Impossible ? That is the word of a fool.

—NAPOLEON I

Every beginning is hard.

—GERMAN PROVERB

The tree is not felled by the first blow.

—FRENCH PROVERB

A word grows to a thought, a thought
to an idea, an idea to an act.
The change is slow, and the present
is a sluggish traveler loafing
in the path tomorrow wants to take.

—BERYL MARKHAM

Find a path or make one.

—SENECA

A journey of a thousand miles
began with a single step.

—LAO-TSE

Step by step one goes very far.

—FRENCH PROVERB

It is only the first step
which is troublesome.

—MME. MARIE DU DEFFAND

What saves a man is to take a step.
Then another step. It is always the
same step, but you have to take it.

—ANTOINE DE SAINT-EXUPÉRY

Every noble activity makes room
for itself.

—EMERSON

Choose always the way that
seems the best, however rough
it may be; custom will soon
render it easy and agreeable.

—PYTHAGORAS

Wisely and slowly;
they stumble that run fast.

—SHAKESPEARE

Slow and steady wins the race.

—ROBERT LLOYD

Hasten slowly.

—AUGUSTUS CAESAR

Unreasonable haste
is the direct road to error.

—MOLIÈRE

Nothing in haste except to catch fleas.

—FRISIAN PROVERB

This life is a journey.

—ANAXAGORAS

It's not the arrival,
it is the journey which matters.

—MONTAIGNE

The artist finds a greater
pleasure in painting than in
having completed the picture.

—SENECA

Not every end is a goal. The end of a
melody is not its goal; however, if
the melody has not reached its end, it
would also not have reached its goal.
A parable.

—NIETZSCHE

Spring

MAY

Come live with me and be my love,
And we will all the pleasures prove
That valleys, groves, hills, and fields,
Woods or steepy mountain yields.

—CHRISTOPHER MARLOWE

THE SWAIN and his lady ride off to explore earthly paradise. She holds his April green branch as he gazes into her eyes with tender affection. Joining the pair on their romantic journey is a turtledove perched on his wrist. The zodiac sign of Taurus is ruled by Venus possibly explaining the artist's intention in portraying the month of May as the culmination of an affair of the heart.

Maia, an obscure Etruscan earth goddess, gives her name to the final month of spring. As wife of Volcanus or Vulcan, god of fire, Maia gentled his nature and was called *Bona Dea* (Good Goddess) by the Romans. Despite so many pleasing aspects, May was considered a most unlucky time of year to marry. Mythologists surmise this attitude arose from the Roman celebration of the Lemuria (May 9, 11, 13), a festival dedicated to placating the unhappy dead.

The last week in May welcomes the entry of Gemini, the Twins, here depicted as a couple embracing behind a wattle fence. Mercury, god of communication, rules as the element of air replaces solid earth. Spirits rise to the call of the strongest and deepest human emotion: love.

In the meadows, during the month
  of May, have you ever felt this scent
  which conveys to every living thing
  the rapture of mating?

    —HONORÉ DE BALZAC

To live is like to love — all reason
  is against it, and all healthy instinct
  is for it.

    —SAMUEL BUTLER

Love is the earliest of our feelings.

    —BERNARD DE FONTENELLE

All loving emotions, like plants,
  shoot up most rapidly in the
  tempestuous atmosphere of life.

    —JEAN PAUL RICHTER

One touch of nature
  makes the whole world kin.

    —SHAKESPEARE

If you drive nature out with a pitch-
  fork, she will soon find a way back.

    —HORACE

Nature must be eluded or obeyed.
  Nothing can prevail against the true.

    —DENIS DIDEROT

Nature is often hidden; sometimes
  overcome; seldom extinguished.

    —SIR FRANCIS BACON

The greatest pleasure of life is love.

    —SIR WILLIAM TEMPLE

Life is a flower of which
  love is the honey.

    —VICTOR HUGO

It is a beautiful necessity
  of our nature to love something.

    —DOUGLAS JERROLD

You are as prone to love as the sun
is to shine; it being the most
delightful and natural employment
of the soul of man.

—THOMAS TRAHERNE

Familiar acts are beautiful
through love.

—SHELLEY

We are shaped and fashioned
by what we love.

—GOETHE

Love and smoke are two things
which cannot be concealed.

—FRENCH PROVERB

Lovers are fools
but nature makes them so.

—ELBERT G. HUBBARD

Nothing is as varied in nature
as the pleasures of love,
although they are always the same.

—NINON DE L'ENCLOS

Artificial manners vanish the moment
the natural passions are touched.

—MARIA EDGEWORTH

Whatever is unnatural
is untrustworthy.

—BERYL MARKHAM

Things are beautiful if you love them.

—JEAN ANOUILH

All thoughts, all passions, all delights,
Whatever stirs this mortal frame,
All are but ministers of Love,
And feed his sacred flame.

—COLERIDGE

Love in its essence is spiritual fire.

—EMANUEL SWEDENBORG

Love is not consolation, it is light.

—SIMONE WEIL

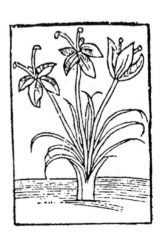

I loved not yet, yet I loved to love.
I sought what I might love,
in love with loving.

—ST. AUGUSTINE

Looks breed love.

—ENGLISH PROVERB

Love looks not with the eyes,
but with the mind.

—SHAKESPEARE

To speak of love is to make love.

—HONORÉ DE BALZAC

Love must be fostered
with soft words.

—OVID

Speak low, if you speak love.

—SHAKESPEARE

True love is best by silence known.

—VOLTAIRE

Never seek to tell thy love,
Love that never told can be;
For the gentle wind doth move
Silently, invisibly.

—WILLIAM BLAKE

It is better to be silent than to say
things at the wrong time that are
too tender; what was appropriate
ten seconds ago is no longer, and
hurts one's cause rather than helps it.

—STENDHAL

Silence is the language of all strong
passions: love, anger, surprise, fear.

—GIACOMO LEOPARDI

It is difficult for a woman
  to define her feelings in language
  which is chiefly made by man
  to express theirs.

—THOMAS HARDY

Men are deceived about women
  because that they forget
  that they and women do not speak
  the same language.

—HENRI FRÉDÉRIC AMIEL

There are three things that I have
  always loved and never understood —
  painting, music, and women.

—BERNARD DE FONTENELLE

A man must choose between
  loving women and knowing them.

—NINON DE L'ENCLOS

Until I truly loved, I was alone.

—CAROLINE NORTON

There has never been a woman yet in
  the world who wouldn't have given
  the top of the milk jug to some man,
  if she had met the right one.

—LADY JANE WILDE

Love is the whole history
  of a woman's life;
  it is but an episode in a man's.

—MME. DE STAËL

Every woman would rather be
  beautiful than good.

—GERMAN PROVERB

A woman despises a man for loving
  her, unless she returns his love.

—ELIZABETH STODDARD

Heaven has no rage, like love
  to hatred turned, nor Hell a fury,
  like a woman scorned.

—WILLIAM CONGREVE

There is no remedy for love
  but to love more.

—THOREAU

Is it what we love, or how we love,
  that makes love good?

—GEORGE ELIOT

Love is the strange bewilderment
  which overtakes one person
  on account of another person.

—JAMES THURBER & E. B WHITE

Whoever loved
  that loved not at first sight?

—CHRISTOPHER MARLOWE

Love that springs into being
  in a moment takes the
  longest time to cure.

—JEAN DE LA BRUYÈRE

The meeting of two personalities
  is like the contact of two chemical
  substances: if there is any reaction,
  both are transformed.

—CARL G. JUNG

Intimates are predestined.

—HENRY ADAMS

Love consists in this,
  that two solitudes protect
  and touch and greet each other.

—RILKE

Love does not consist in gazing
  at each other but in looking outward
  together in the same direction.

—ANTOINE DE SAINT-EXUPÉRY

Nothing is less in our power than
  the heart and far from commanding
  we are forced to obey it.

—JEAN JACQUES ROUSSEAU

In wise love each divines
  the high secret self of the other,
  and, refusing to believe in the mere
  daily self, creates a mirror where
  the lover or the beloved sees an
  image to copy in daily life.

—WILLIAM BUTLER YEATS

I hate and I love: why I do so
  you may well ask. I do not know,
  but I feel it happen and am in agony.

—CATULLUS

Love makes everything lovely;
  hate concentrates itself
  on the one thing hated.

—GEORGE MACDONALD

Of all the objects of hatred, a woman
  once loved is the most hateful.

—MAX BEERBOHM

Delicacy is to love
what grace is to beauty.

—MME. DE MAINTENON

Love lessens woman's delicacy
and increases man's.

—JEAN PAUL RICHTER

Love is but the heart's immortal thirst
to be completely known
and all forgiven.

—HENRY VAN DYKE

Judged by most of its results, love is
closer to hatred than to friendship.

—LA ROCHEFOUCAULD

Whereas love is of itself a reward and
an object worth striving for, personal
hatred has no triumphs that are
not trivial, secondary and human.

—OLIVE MOORE

Hatred comes from the heart;
contempt from the head; and neither
feeling is quite within our control.

—SCHOPENHAUER

Friendship is far more magic than love.
It lasts longer.

—OSCAR WILDE

Friendship is a disinterested
commerce between equals;
love, an abject intercourse
between tyrants and slaves.

—OLIVER GOLDSMITH

Friendship is love without his wings!

—LORD BYRON

Friendship often ends in love;
but love, in friendship—never.

—CHARLES CALEB COLTON

Hatred is easy to conceal,
love difficult, indifference
the most difficult of all.

—JULES RENARD

The worst sin towards our fellow
creatures is not to hate them,
but to be indifferent to them;
that's the essence of inhumanity.

—GEORGE BERNARD SHAW

Love is a pleasing but a various clime.

—WILLIAM SHENSTONE

Love slays what we have been
that we may be what we were not.

—ST. AUGUSTINE

Most people would rather
get than give affection.

—ARISTOTLE

Selfishness is one of the qualities
apt to inspire love.

—NATHANIEL HAWTHORNE

To love but little is in love an
infallible means of being beloved.

—LA ROCHEFOUCAULD

If she would reign long,
let her scorn her lover.

—OVID

An absence, the decline of a
dinner invitation, an unintentional
coldness, can accomplish more
than all the cosmetics and
beautiful dresses in the world.

—MARCEL PROUST

The less my hope the hotter my love.

—TERENCE

Advantages are lawful in love and war.

—APHRA BEHN

Love is a kind of warfare.

—OVID

The only victory over love is flight.

—NAPOLEON I

Of all the thirty-six alternatives,
running away is best.

—CHINESE PROVERB

Love sought is good
  but given unsought is better.

—SHAKESPEARE

He who asks fearfully invites denial.

—SENECA

If you have to ask,
  then the answer is no.

—MARTHA GRAHAM

No answer is also an answer.

—GERMAN PROVERB

Kindness is in our power,
  but fondness is not.

—SAMUEL JOHNSON

It is kindness not to excite hopes
  that must end in disappointment.

—PUBLILIUS SYRUS

A part of kindness consists in
  loving people more than they deserve.

—JOSEPH JOUBERT

Faults are thick where love is thin.

—ENGLISH PROVERB

Analysis kills love,
  as well as other things.

—JOHN BROWN

No human creature
  can give orders to love.

—GEORGE SAND

The magic of our first love
  is the ignorance that it can ever end.

—DISRAELI

The terror as well as the beauty
  of love lies in the fact
  that it alters all values.

—UNA POPE-HENNESSY

In fool's paradise
  there is room for many lovers.

—SAMUEL HOPKINS ADAMS

Love is space and time
  measured by the heart.

—MARCEL PROUST

Our hours in love have wings;
  in absence, crutches.

—COLLEY CIBBER

A crowd is not company,
  and faces are but a gallery of pictures,
  and talk but a tinkling cymbal
  where there is no love.

—SIR FRANCIS BACON

Absence sharpens love;
  presence strengthens it.

—THOMAS FULLER

Absence diminishes moderate passions
  and increases great ones,
  as the wind extinguishes tapers
  and adds fury to fire.

—LA ROCHEFOUCAULD

Love reckons hours for months,
  and days for years; and
  every little absence is an age.

—JOHN DRYDEN

Sometimes when one person is missing,
  the whole world seems depopulated.

—LAMARTINE

Absences are a good influence in love
  and keep it bright and delicate.

—ROBERT LOUIS STEVENSON

All who joy would win must
  share it — happiness was born a twin.

—LORD BYRON

Can there be a love which does not
  make demands on its object?

—CONFUCIUS

Those who shun love altogether
  are as foolish as those
  who pursue it too diligently.

—EURIPIDES

Seek not happiness too greedily,
  and be not fearful of unhappiness.

—LAO-TZE

The pursuit of happiness is a most
  ridiculous phrase; if you pursue
  happiness you'll never find it.

—C. P. SNOW

The rapture of pursuing is the prize.

—LONGFELLOW

An object in possession
  seldom retains the same charm
  that it had in pursuit.

—PLINY THE YOUNGER

In every passionate pursuit, the pursuit
  counts more than the object pursued.

—ERIC HOFFER

Pursuits pass over into habits.

—OVID

Most affections are habits or duties
  we lack the courage to end.

—HENRI DE MONTHERLANT

The chains of habit are
  too weak to be felt until
  they are too strong to be broken.

—SAMUEL JOHNSON

By habit love enters the mind;
  by habit is love unlearnt.

—OVID

There is no heaven like mutual love.

—GEORGE GRANVILLE

Love is worthless if it is not mutual.

—MARIE DE FRANCE

Need not who needs not thee.

—BASQUE PROVERB

All sorrows can be borne
 if you put them into a story
 or tell a story about them.

—ISAK DINESEN

'Tis better to have loved and lost,
Than never to have loved at all.

—ALFRED, LORD TENNYSON

They who lose today
 may win tomorrow.

—CERVANTES

What's gone and what's past help
 should be past grief.

—SHAKESPEARE

Between grief and nothing
 I will take grief.

—WILLIAM FAULKNER

All love is vanquished
 by a succeeding love.

—OVID

Our will is always
 for our own good, but
 we do not always see what that is.

—JEAN JACQUES ROUSSEAU

We are all born for love;
 it is the principle of existence
 and its only end.

—DISRAELI

Were it not for love poor life would
 be a ship not worth the launching.

—EDWIN ARLINGTON ROBINSON

Old and young,
 we are all on our last cruise.

—ROBERT LOUIS STEVENSON

Summer

JUNE

A little learning is a dangerous thing;
Drink deep, or taste not the Pierian spring:
There shallow draughts intoxicate the brain,
And drinking largely sobers us again.

—ALEXANDER POPE

THIS MONTH'S name may derive from the ancient Italian goddess Juno. Jupiter's consort had a far more agreeable disposition than her Greek counterpart, the jealous and scheming Hera. With dignity befitting the Queen of Heaven, Juno protected matrimony and looked after the welfare of women from birth to death. The Romans celebrated her major festival in June regarding this time of year as most fortunate for weddings. A marriage in June is "good to the man and happy to the maid," according to one old Latin text.

Gemini's Twins, Castor and Pollux, are pictured here nestled in the clouds, for Jupiter made them stars in reward for their brotherly devotion. Quick-witted Mercury reigns till summer solstice when the sun reaches its zenith. Cancer's Crab, a dreamy water sign governed by the moon, takes over the remaining days of June.

The seasonal Books of Days most often symbolized June with scenes of sheep shearing, a principal rural labor in early summer. The sun's retreat prompted thoughts of impending winter when wool spun into cloth would afford protection against the cold: foresight was essential in medieval society.

Providing for the future by sound and sensible means has ever been a human requirement. Beyond its obvious necessity, learning is surely one of the most satisfying of life's endeavors.

An aim in life is the
only fortune worth finding.

-ROBERT LOUIS STEVENSON

There is no meaning to life except
the meaning man gives his life
by the unfolding of his powers.

-ERICH FROMM

The only difference between one man
and another — between the weak and
the powerful, the great and the
insignificant — is energy; invincible
determination; a purpose once
formed and then death or victory.

-SIR THOMAS BUXTON

All life, even in its lowest form,
is energy.

-PLOTINUS

This world belongs to the energetic.

-EMERSON

Every individual has a place
to fill in the world, and is
important in some respect,
whether he chooses to be so or not.

-NATHANIEL HAWTHORNE

Only actions give to life its strength,
as only moderation gives it its charm.

-JEAN PAUL RICHTER

Activity is the only road to knowledge.

-GEORGE BERNARD SHAW

The good life is one inspired by love
and guided by knowledge.

-BERTRAND RUSSELL

Knowledge itself is power.

—SIR FRANCIS BACON

It does not make much difference
what a person studies — all knowledge
is related, and the man who
studies anything, if he keeps at it,
will become learned.

—HYPATIA

The happiest life is that which
constantly exercises and educates
what is best in us.

—PHILIP G. HAMERTON

Every day that we spend without
learning something is a day lost.

—BEETHOVEN

The triumph of learning is that it
leaves something done solidly forever.

—VIRGINIA WOOLF

They know enough
who know how to learn.

—HENRY ADAMS

Education is an ornament in prosperity
and a refuge in adversity.

—ARISTOTLE

Education is a possession
that none can take away.

—MENANDER

Training is everything. The peach
was once a bitter almond;
cauliflower is nothing but
cabbage with a college education.

—MARK TWAIN

Cultivation is as necessary to the mind
as food is to the body.

—CICERO

The richest soil, if uncultivated,
produces the rankest weeds.

—PLUTARCH

The soil, however rich it may be,
cannot be productive without
culture, so the mind, without cultivation, can never produce good fruit.

—SENECA

The roots of education are bitter,
but the fruit is sweet.

—ARISTOTLE

'Tis education forms the common
mind, just as the twig is bent,
the tree's inclin'd.

—ALEXANDER POPE

Learning is no child's play;
  we cannot learn without pain.

—ARISTOTLE

The gem cannot be polished
  without friction, nor man perfected
  without trials.

—CHINESE PROVERB

Compulsion must be used with the
  mind to impel it to exertion.

—SENECA

It is impossible for anyone
  to begin to learn what he
  thinks he already knows.

—EPICTETUS

Some will never learn anything,
  for this reason, because they
  understand everything too soon.

—SIR THOMAS POPE BLOUNT

Practice is the best of all instructors.

—PUBLILIUS SYRUS

Practice is everything.

—PERIANDER

One must learn by doing the thing;
  though you think you know it,
  you have no certainty until you try.

—SOPHOCLES

I hear and I forget.
I see and I remember.
I do and I understand.

—CHINESE PROVERB

We never do anything well
  till we cease to think about
  the manner of doing it.

—WILLIAM HAZLITT

Nothing is so difficult that it cannot
  be accomplished by diligence.

—TERENCE

Learning makes a man
  fit company for himself.

—EDWARD YOUNG

One of the earliest lessons I learned
  as a child was that if you looked away
  from something, it might not
  be there when you looked back.

   —JOHN EDGAR WIDEMAN

We do not really know
  anything at all until a long time
  after we have learned it.

   —JOSEPH JOUBERT

It is not enough to have a good mind.
  The main thing is to use it well.

   —DESCARTES

One must learn to think well
  before learning to think;
  afterward it proves too difficult.

   —ANATOLE FRANCE

Education is that which discloses to the
  wise and disguises from the foolish
  their lack of understanding.

   —AMBROSE BIERCE

Real education must ultimately be
  limited to one who insists on knowing, the rest is mere sheep-herding.

   —EZRA POUND

What we want is to see the child
  in pursuit of knowledge, and not
  knowledge in pursuit of the child.

   —GEORGE BERNARD SHAW

The authority of those who teach
  is often an obstacle to those
  who want to learn.

   —CICERO

The surest way to corrupt a young man
  is to teach him to esteem more highly
  those who think alike than those
  who think differently.

—NIETZSCHE

Teachers open the door.
  You enter by yourself.

—CHINESE PROVERB

The first thing education teaches you
  is to walk alone.

—ANONYMOUS

I advise the young to tell themselves
  constantly that most often
  it is up to them alone.

—ANDRÉ GIDE

Compared to what we ought to be,
  we are only half awake. We are
  making use of only a small part
  of our physical and mental resources.

—WILLIAM JAMES

It was a high counsel which I
  once heard given to a young person:
  Always do what you are afraid to do.

—EMERSON

We must never be afraid to go too far,
  for truth lies beyond.

—MARCEL PROUST

The brighter you are
  the more you have to learn.

—DON HEROLD

Think wrongly, if you please;
  but in all cases think for yourself.

—BRUNO LESSING

We think too small. Like the frog
  at the bottom of the well. He thinks
  the sky is only as big as the top
  of the well. If he surfaced, he would
  have an entirely different view.

—MAO TSE-TUNG

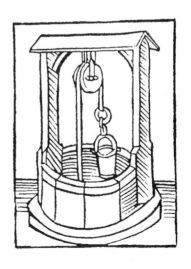

People have one thing in common;
  they are all different.

> —ROBERT ZEND

The more peculiarly his own a man's
  character is, the better it fits him.

> —CICERO

We forfeit three-fourths of ourselves
  in order to be like other people.

> —SCHOPENHAUER

When people are free to do
  as they please, they usually
  imitate other people.

> —ERIC HOFFER

To be nobody but yourself in a world
  which is doing its best, night and day,
  to make you somebody else — means
  to fight the hardest battle which
  any human being can fight;
  and never stop fighting.

> —E. E. CUMMINGS

It is a blessed thing that in every age
  someone has the individuality
  enough and the courage enough
  to stand by his own convictions.

> —ROBERT G. INGERSOLL

Very few are able to raise themselves
  above the ideas of their times.

> —VOLTAIRE

People seldom improve
  when they have no model
  but themselves to copy after.

> —OLIVER GOLDSMITH

Example is the school of mankind;
  they will learn at no other.

> —EDMUND BURKE

Tell me to what you pay attention
  and I will tell you who you are.

> —ORTEGA Y GASSET

How can you come to know yourself?
  Never by thinking; always by doing.

> —GOETHE

Learning without thought is labor lost;
thought without learning is perilous.

—CONFUCIUS

We live and learn
but not the wiser grow.

—JOHN POMFRET

To live for a time close to great minds
is the best kind of education.

—SIR JOHN BUCHAN

Reflect on the Greek philosophers
and study them night and day.

—HORACE

I assure you I had rather excel others in
the knowledge of what is excellent,
than in the extent of my power
and dominion.

—ALEXANDER THE GREAT

No single event can awaken within us
a stranger totally unknown to us.
To live is to be slowly born.

—ANTOINE DE SAINT-EXUPÉRY

He who would learn to fly one day
must first learn to stand and walk
and run and climb and dance,
one cannot fly into flying.

—NIETZSCHE

I know of no more encouraging fact
than the unquestionable ability
of man to elevate his life
by a conscious endeavor.

—THOREAU

Not to go back, is somewhat
to advance, and men must walk
at least before they dance.

—ALEXANDER POPE

He only is advancing in life whose
heart is getting softer, whose blood
warmer, whose brain quicker, whose
spirit is entering into living peace.

—JOHN RUSKIN

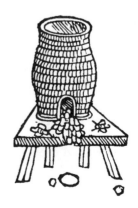

Time is the school in which we learn,
time is the fire in which we burn.

—DELMORE SCHWARTZ

Lost time is never found again.

—BENJAMIN FRANKLIN

Life is short, the craft so long to learn,
opportunities fleeting, experience
treacherous, judgement difficult.

—HIPPOCRATES

We must learn two things from
experience: to correct a great deal,
and not to correct too much.

—EUGÈNE DELACROIX

You never know what is
enough, unless you know what
is more than enough.

—WILLIAM BLAKE

Hold to the now, the here, through
which all future plunges to the past.

—JAMES JOYCE

The goal of yesterday will be
the starting point of tomorrow.

—THOMAS CARLYLE

Time is the soul of this world.

—PYTHAGORAS

Time is infinite movement
without one moment of rest.

—TOLSTOY

Life is one long process
of getting tired.

—SAMUEL BUTLER

The desire of knowledge, like
the thirst of riches, increases ever
with the acquisition of it.

—LAURENCE STERNE

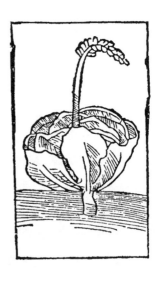

Our life's a stage, a playground;
  learn to play and take nought
seriously, or bear its troubles.

—PALLADAS

Ease and relaxation are profitable to
  all studies. The mind is like a bow,
the stronger by being unbent.

—BEN JONSON

Nothing will take the place of
  persevering study — to it alone
the secret of life delivers itself.

—RODIN

What you think you must do
  is what you want to do.

—MARIE VON EBNER-ESCHENBACH

What we learn with pleasure
  we never forget.

—ALFRED MERCIER

No profit grows where there is
  no pleasure taken; in brief, sir,
study what you most affect.

—SHAKESPEARE

No man can read with profit
  that which he cannot learn
to read with pleasure.

—NOAH PORTER

Some books are to be tasted,
  others to be swallowed, and some few
to be chewed and digested.

—SIR FRANCIS BACON

Know how to prefer
  what costs you the most effort.

—ANDRÉ GIDE

The test of a vocation is
  the love of the drudgery it involves.

—LOGAN PEARSALL SMITH

What is now proved was once
only imagined.

—WILLIAM BLAKE

He who has imagination without
learning has wings and no feet.

—JOSEPH JOUBERT

The more we study,
the more we discover our ignorance.

—SHELLEY

Whoever would be cured of ignorance
must confess it.

—MONTAIGNE

Ignorance is the night of the mind,
but a night without moon or stars.

—CONFUCIUS

Seeking to know is only
too often learning to doubt.

—MME. DESHOULIÈRES

Only the fools are certain and assured.
For doubting pleases me no less
than knowing.

—DANTE

Every mystery solved brings us
to the threshold of a greater one.

—RACHEL CARSON

Curiosity is one of the
permanent and certain characteristics
of a vigorous intellect.

—SAMUEL JOHNSON

Curiosity has its own reason for
existence. The important thing
is not to stop questioning.

—ALBERT EINSTEIN

The man who is afraid of asking
is ashamed of learning.

—DANISH PROVERB

The man who fears nothing
is as powerful as he
who is feared by everybody.

—SCHILLER

Let ignorance talk as it will,
learning has its value.

—LA FONTAINE

Do what you can with what you have,
  where you are.

—THEODORE ROOSEVELT

The world is before you
  and you need not take it or leave it
  as it was when you came in.

—JAMES BALDWIN

Oft-times nothing profits more
  than self-esteem, grounded on
  just and right well-managed.

—JOHN MILTON

Remember, no one can make you
  feel inferior without your consent.

—ELEANOR ROOSEVELT

To be happy we must not
  be too concerned with others.

—ALBERT CAMUS

It matters not what you are
  thought to be, but what you are.

—PUBLILIUS SYRUS

No man is a failure
  who is enjoying life.

—WILLIAM FEATHER

All serious daring starts from within.

—EUDORA WELTY

Without optimism
  there can be no vitality.

—SIR JOHN BUCHAN

It is certainly wrong to despair;
  and if despair is wrong hope is right.

—SIR JOHN LUBBOCK

Whatever enlarges hope
  will also exalt courage.

—SAMUEL JOHNSON

Hope saves a man
  in the midst of misfortunes.

—MENANDER

Work and hope. But never hope
  more than you work.

—BERYL MARKHAM

Summer

JULY

A thing of beauty is a joy forever:
Its loveliness increases; it will never
Pass into nothingness; but still will keep
A bower quiet for us, and a sleep
Full of sweet dreams, and health, and quiet breathing.

—JOHN KEATS

MONTHS V through X were numbered rather than named in the ancient Roman scheme of time. But the fifth month known as *Quintillis* became *Julius* or July in 44 B.C. to honor the memory of the great Julius Caesar, for it was his birth month. Before his assassination earlier in that year, Caesar had reorganized the calendar with help from the Greek astronomer Sosigenes. The Julian system lasted until 1582 when Pope Gregory instituted the current calendar year.

The long hot days of summer are astrologically assigned to Earth's primary luminaries — the moon and the sun. The gentle Crab of Cancer is followed by the fierce Leo the Lion whose ruler is the sun. According to the old precept of *as above, so below*: a growing period governed by the moon — shining on light borrowed from the sun — is replaced by the powerful sun itself as the crop is harvested.

"Make hay while the sun shines" could be the title for the woodcut illustrating July. Mowing, drying, and piling grass in stacks will provide barn fodder for livestock during the barren winter. These are days of promise and fulfillment appropriate to speculation on the nature of happiness.

The great and only serious business
of life is to live happily.

—VOLTAIRE

Happiness consists in this — that a man
can preserve his own being.

—SPINOZA

What man strives to preserve,
in preserving himself, is something
which he has never been at
any particular moment.

—GEORGE SANTAYANA

Man is an animal and his happiness
depends on his physiology
more than he likes to think.

—BERTRAND RUSSELL

It is not the place, nor the condition,
but the mind alone that can
make anyone happy or miserable.

—SIR ROGER L'ESTRANGE

You stop being happy as soon
as you are conscious of wanting to be
happy. Happiness, like health,
must be unconscious.

—BERNARD DE FONTENELLE

Health of body and mind
is a great blessing, if we can bear it.

—CARDINAL JOHN NEWMAN

What is always speaking silently
is the body.

—NORMAN O. BROWN

The body, a true path to culture,
teaches us where our limits lie.

—ALBERT CAMUS

The body has its end which
it does not know; the mind its means
of which it is unaware.

—PAUL VALÉRY

You have to believe in happiness
or happiness never comes.

—DOUGLAS MALLOCH

He is not happy who does
not think himself so.

—PUBLILIUS SYRUS

It is a great obstacle to happiness
to expect too much.

—BERNARD DE FONTENELLE

The bird of paradise alights only
upon the hand that does not grasp.

—JOHN, DUKE OF BERRY

It is preoccupation with possession,
more than anything else, that prevents
man from living freely and nobly.

—BERTRAND RUSSELL

He who binds to himself a Joy
Doth the winged life destroy;
But he who kisses the Joy as it flies
Lives in Eternity's sunrise.

—WILLIAM BLAKE

Perfect happiness, even in memory,
is not common.

—JANE AUSTEN

Perfect happiness is the absence of
striving for happiness; perfect renown
is the absence of concern for renown.

—CHUANG-TSE

There is nothing vainer
than the love of fame.

—THEOPHRASTUS

What is fame? The advantage
of being known by people of
whom you know nothing,
and for whom you care as little.

—KING STANISLAS OF POLAND

He who seeks only for applause
from without has all his happiness
in another's keeping.

—OLIVER GOLDSMITH

Applause is the spur of noble minds,
the end and aim of weak ones.

—CHARLES CALEB COLTON

The excessive desire of pleasing
goes along almost always with the
apprehension of not being liked.

—THOMAS FULLER

There is no rule more invariable than
that we are paid for our suspicions
by finding what we suspected.

—THOREAU

Above all things, never think
that you're not good enough
yourself. A man should never think
that. My belief is that in life
people will take you very much
at your own reckoning.

—ANTHONY TROLLOPE

Who will adhere to him
that abandons himself?

—SIR PHILIP SIDNEY

That kind of life is most happy which
affords us the most opportunities
of gaining our own esteem.

—SAMUEL JOHNSON

What others think of us would
be of little moment did it not,
when known, so deeply tinge
what we think of ourselves.

—GEORGE SANTAYANA

Our opinion of others is not so variable
as our opinion of ourselves.

—VAUVENARGUES

We are all apt to believe
what the world believes about us.

—GEORGE ELIOT

One is happy in the world only
when one forgets the world.

—ANATOLE FRANCE

Comparison, more than reality,
makes men happy, and
can make them wretched.

—OWEN FELTHAM

To be content with what we possess
is the greatest and most secure
of all riches.

—CICERO

He that fails in his endeavors after
wealth or power will not long retain
either honesty or courage.

—SAMUEL JOHNSON

Where ambition ends, happiness begins.

—HUNGARIAN PROVERB

Happiness is not a reward — it is
a consequence. Suffering is not
a punishment — it is a result.

—RALPH INGERSOLL

If you imagine that once you have
accomplished your ambitions you
will have time to turn to the Way,
you will discover that your ambitions
never come to an end.

—YOSHIDA KENKO

We cannot seek or attain health,
wealth, learning, justice or kindness
in general. Action is always specific,
concrete, individualized, unique.

—JOHN DEWEY

The future enters into us,
in order to transform itself in us,
long before it happens.

—RILKE

Experience teaches us that it is
no more in our power to have
a sound mind, than a sound body.

—SPINOZA

Every luxury must be paid for,
and everything is a luxury,
starting with being in the world.

—CESARE PAVESE

There are two things to aim at in life:
first, to get what you want; and,
after that, to enjoy it. Only the
wisest of mankind achieve the second.

—LOGAN PEARSALL SMITH

The art of being wise is the art
of knowing what to overlook.

—WILLIAM JAMES

To insure peace of mind
ignore the rules and regulations.

—GEORGE ADE

Oh, if only we could get used to
living without dogmatic principles,
what a progress that would be!

—GUSTAVE FLAUBERT

Dogma does not mean the absence
of thought, but the end of thought.

—G. K. CHESTERTON

Life is a rose that withers
in the iron fist of dogma.

—GEORGE MOORE

The first and great commandment is:
Don't let them scare you.

—ELMER DAVIS

The great pleasure in life is doing
what people say you cannot do.

—WALTER BAGEHOT

An individual has only to refuse to
play the game of existence according
to the current rules to throw the
rule-observing players into bewildered
consternation. They are appalled,
they are at a loss, they are helpless.

—ALDOUS HUXLEY

Life is a quarry out of which
we have to mould and chisel
and complete a character.

—GOETHE

Each man's character
shapes his fortune.

—CORNELIUS NEPOS

Know thyself; this is the great object.

—SENECA

It is the chiefest point of happiness
that a man is willing to be what he is.

—ERASMUS

The affirmation of one's essential
being in spite of desires and anxieties
creates joy.

—PAUL TILLICH

To the possession of the self
the way is inward.

—PLOTINUS

The wise man looks for what is within,
the fool for what is without.

—CONFUCIUS

As you are, so you wish and hope.

—JOHANN KASPAR LAVATER

I gratefully enjoy what comes from
the outside but depend on nothing.

—KARL WILHELM VON HUMBOLDT

Hope is a much greater stimulant
of life than any happiness.

—NIETZSCHE

Hope is itself a species of happiness,
and perhaps the chief happiness
which this world affords.

—SAMUEL JOHNSON

Hope is a borrowing from happiness.

—JOSEPH JOUBERT

Welcome everything
that comes to you, but
do not long for anything else.

—ANDRÉ GIDE

Things are where things are,
and, as fate has willed,
so shall they be fulfilled.

—AESCHYLUS

Everything comes gradually
and at its appointed hour.

—OVID

A sip is the most that mortals are
permitted from any goblet of delight.

—AMOS BRONSON ALCOTT

The difficulty in life is the choice.

—GEORGE MOORE

The more alternatives,
the more difficult the choice.

—ABBÉ D'ALLAINVAL

Think long when you may
decide only once.

—PUBLILIUS SYRUS

Half of our mistakes in life arise from
feeling where we ought to think,
and thinking where we ought to feel.

—JOHN CHURTON COLLINS

The world is a comedy to those that
think, a tragedy to those who feel.

—HORACE WALPOLE

Chance decides matters
  better than ourselves.

—MENANDER

The two greatest tyrants on earth;
  chance and time.

—JOHANN VON HERDER

Take what you can use
  and let the rest go by.

—KEN KESEY

One cannot collect all the
  beautiful shells on the beach.

—ANNE MORROW LINDBERGH

Experience has taught me this, that
  we undo ourselves by impatience.
  Misfortunes have their life and their
  limits, their sickness and their health.

—MONTAIGNE

There's more to life
  than increasing its speed.

—GANDHI

For no one does life drag
  more disagreeably than
  for him who tries to speed it up.

—JEAN PAUL RICHTER

Man is fond of counting his troubles
  but he does not count his joys.
  If he counted them up as he ought to,
  he would see that every lot
  has enough happiness provided for it.

—DOSTOYEVSKY

Nature has given the opportunity
  of happiness to all, knew they
  but how to use it.

—CLAUDIAN

The unhappiness of man
  is due to his ignorance of nature.

—BARON PAUL D'HOLBACH

We all look at nature too much,
  and live with her too little.

—OSCAR WILDE

The love of nature is the only love
that does not deceive human hopes.

     —HONORÉ DE BALZAC

Look deep into nature and you will
find the answer to everything.

     —ALBERT EINSTEIN

The more I see of life the more I
perceive that only through solitary
communion with nature can one gain
an idea of its richness and meaning.

     —CYRIL CONNOLLY

The greatest delight which fields
and woods minister is the suggestion
of an occult relation between
man and vegetable. I am not alone
and unacknowledged. They nod to
me, and I to them.

     —EMERSON

Art is embedded in nature
and he who can extract it, has it.

     —ALBRECHT DÜRER

Art is a human activity having
for its purpose the transmission to
others of the highest and best feelings
to which men have risen.

     —TOLSTOY

Artists do not prove things. They
do not need to. They know them.

     —GEORGE BERNARD SHAW

Nothing is more useful to man
than those arts which have no utility.

     —OVID

Music is essentially useless, as life is.

     —GEORGE SANTAYANA

Without music life would be a mistake.

—NIETZSCHE

Music is a higher revelation
  than philosophy.

—BEETHOVEN

Music produces a kind of pleasure
  which human nature
  cannot do without.

—CONFUCIUS

One half of the world cannot
  understand the pleasures of the other.

—JANE AUSTEN

Every generation is a secret society
  and has incommunicable enthusiasms,
  tastes, and interests which are a
  mystery both to its predecessors
  and to posterity.

—JOHN JAY CHAPMAN

Put only this restriction on your
  pleasures: be cautious that they
  hurt no creature that has life.

—JOHANN VON ZIMMERMAN

Pleasure is not happiness.
  It has no more importance
  than a shadow following a man.

—MUHAMMAD ALI

Pleasure is very seldom found where
it is sought. Our brightest blazes
of gladness are commonly kindled
by unexpected sparks.

—SAMUEL JOHNSON

The only thing worth having in an
earthly existence is a sense of humor.

—LINCOLN STEFFENS

In merciless and rollicking comedy
life is caught in the act.

—GEORGE SANTAYANA

You can pretend to be serious;
you can't pretend to be witty.

—SACHA GUITRY

If you can't be funny, be interesting.

—HAROLD ROSS

When a thing is funny,
search it for a hidden truth.

—GEORGE BERNARD SHAW

The faculty of laughter
is not in the brain but in the heart.

—LAURENT JOUBERT

Go to your bosom; knock there,
and ask your heart what it doth know.

—SHAKESPEARE

There is no instinct
like that of the heart.

—LORD BYRON

The heart is an astrologer
that always divines the truth.

—CONFUCIUS

Mind is the partial side of man;
the heart is everything.

—ANTOINE RIVAROL

The door to happiness opens outwards.

—KIERKEGAARD

Happiness seems made to be shared.

—CORNEILLE

I never have a merry thought without
being vexed at having to keep it to
myself, with nobody to share it.

—MONTAIGNE

Of all the things which wisdom
provides to make life entirely
happy, much the greatest
is the possession of friendship.

—EPICURUS

True happiness consists
  not in the multitude of friends,
  but in the worth and choice.

—BEN JONSON

The first duty of friendship
  is to leave your friend his illusions.

—ARTHUR SCHNITZLER

Nothing is more sad
  than the death of an illusion.

—ARTHUR KOESTLER

To become mature is to recover
  that sense of seriousness which
  one had as a child at play.

—NIETZSCHE

A great man is he who has
  not lost the heart of a child.

—MENCIUS

We ought to be happy without
  thinking too much of being so.

—FRENCH PROVERB

Happiness makes up in height
  for what it lacks in length.

—ROBERT FROST

Happiness is a mystery, like religion,
  and should never be rationalized.

—G. K. CHESTERTON

Youth is a time of illusion;
  but that is because it sees things
  as infinitely less lovable, abundant
  and desirable than they are:
  age cures us of this misunderstanding.

—PAUL CLAUDEL

Truth is within ourselves.

—ROBERT BROWNING

Truth is always straightforward.

—SOPHOCLES

The language of truth is simple.

—EURIPIDES

Truth is always paradoxical.

—THOREAU

The truth is that life is delicious,
  horrible, charming, frightful, sweet,
  bitter, and that is everything.

—ANATOLE FRANCE

It will not be always summer,
  therefore fill thy barns.

—HESIOD

Summer

AUGUST

Cruelty has a human heart,
And jealousy a human face;
Terror, the human form divine,
And secrecy, the human dress.

—WILLIAM BLAKE

UGUSTUS CAESAR, on his death bed asked, "Have I acted out the comedy well?" Highest praise for his performance is due the first and greatest Roman emperor. His peaceful reign saw the Golden Age of Roman literature, the establishment of public libraries, and the transformation of the city of Rome from humble brick into a splendid marble testament to its greatness. *Sextilis*, the sixth month, became *Augustus* with the emperor's consent, for within its time span many triumphs and other fortunate events of his life had occurred.

Our rural calendar depicts the harvest of grain — the work begins under the auspices of the sun and the Lion; ending as the discriminating Virgin and her ruler, the artful Mercury, take over. The astrological Virgo traditionally holds a sheaf of wheat identifying her with the earth and its produce.

Threshing, the act of separating the wheat from chaff, follows the harvest and in life as well as on the farm it is essential to discern the difference between the worthwhile and the worthless. A medieval concept — the Seven Deadly Sins — defines human vices as greed, envy, lust, anger, pride, sloth, and gluttony. Time has added to the list.

Avarice, envy, pride,
  Three fatal sparks.

—DANTE

There is no vice which mankind
  carries to such wild extremes
  as that of avarice.

—JONATHAN SWIFT

The bounty of nature is too little
  for the greedy man.

—SENECA

He who doesn't find a little enough,
  will find nothing enough.

—EPICURUS

There is a sufficiency in the world for
  man's need but not for man's greed.

—GANDHI

Envy, the meanest of vices,
  creeps on the ground like a serpent.

—OVID

He who envies admits his inferiority.

—LATIN PROVERB

As iron is eaten away by rust
  so the envious are consumed
  by their own passion.

—ANTISTHENES

Envy, among other ingredients,
  has a mixture of love of justice in it.
  We are more angry at undeserved
  than at deserved good fortune.

—WILLIAM HAZLITT

Towers are measured by their
  shadows, and men of merit
  by those who are envious of them.

—CHINESE PROVERB

One of the few benefits of
  growing older is that envy
  is replaced by admiration.

—JAMES POPE-HENNESSEY

Every ambitious man is a captive
and every covetous one a pauper.

—ARAB PROVERB

Covetousness bursts the sack
and spills the grain.

—SIR WALTER SCOTT

The covetous man is full of fear;
and he who lives in fear
will ever be a bondsman.

—HORACE

A man is rich in proportion to
the things he can afford to let alone.

—THOREAU

We are all inclined to judge ourselves
by our ideals; others by their acts.

—HAROLD NICOLSON

There is perhaps no phenomenon
which contains so much destructive
feeling as moral indignation which
permits envy or hate to be acted out
under the guise of virtue.

—ERICH FROMM

Nothing is more unpleasant than
a virtuous person with a mean mind.

—WALTER BAGEHOT

Pride will have a fall.

—ENGLISH PROVERB

Half of the harm that is done
in this world
Is due to people who want to
feel important.

—T. S. ELIOT

Pride does not wish to owe
and vanity does not wish to pay.

—LA ROCHEFOUCAULD

Self-love seems so often unrequited.

—ANTHONY POWELL

A knowlege of thyself
will preserve thee from vanity.

—CERVANTES

Meanness is incurable; it cannot be
cured by old age, or by anything else.

—ARISTOTLE

Prudery is a kind of avarice,
the worst of all.

—STENDHAL

Moral indignation is
jealousy with a halo.

—H. G. WELLS

Indulgence toward one's self
and sternness towards others
are one and the same vice.

—JEAN DE LA BRUYÈRE

Violent antipathies are always
suspicious, and betray a
secret affinity.

—WILLIAM HAZLITT

Puritanism is the haunting fear
that someone, somewhere,
may be happy.

—H. L. MENCKEN

The greatest of faults is
to be conscious of none.

—THOMAS CARLYLE

The usual pretext of those
who make others unhappy
is that they do it
for their own good.

—VAUVENARGUES

More people are flattered into virtue
than are bullied out of vice.

—R. S. SURTEES

There is a kind of sweetness
of character that stinks.

—BENJAMIN DECASSERES

No people do so much harm
as those who go about
doing good.

—MANDELL CREIGHTON

Virtue has need of limits.

—MONTESQUIEU

There is nothing either good or bad,
but thinking makes it so.

—SHAKESPEARE

We think as we do,
mainly because other people think so.

—SAMUEL BUTLER

Forgive many things in others;
nothing in yourself.

—AUSONIUS

He who excuses himself
accuses himself.

—GABRIEL MEURIER

No one knows what he is doing so long
as he is acting rightly; but of what is
wrong one is always conscious.

—GOETHE

One thing is always wrong — always:
to cause suffering in others for the
purpose of gratifying one's own
pleasure; that is everlastingly wrong.

—LAFCADIO HEARN

Labor to keep alive in your breast
that little spark of celestial fire,
conscience.

—GEORGE WASHINGTON

Nothing is rarer than real goodness.

—LA ROCHEFOUCAULD

Nature does not bestow virtue;
to be good is an art.

—SENECA

No virtue is acquired in an instant,
but step by step.

—ISAAC BARROW

When about to do an evil thing,
though there be no other witness,
respect thyself and forbear.

—AUSONIUS

It is not alone what we do,
but also what we do not do,
for which we are accountable.

—MOLIÈRE

To know what is right and not do it
is the worst cowardice.

—CONFUCIUS

Everyone insists on his innocence, at
all costs, even if it means accusing the
rest of the human race and heaven.

—ALBERT CAMUS

Act nothing in a furious passion;
  it's putting to sea in a storm.

—THOMAS FULLER

The best cure for anger is delay.

—SENECA

To be angry is to revenge
  the fault of others upon ourselves.

—ALEXANDER POPE

If you are patient in one moment
  of anger, you will escape
  a hundred days of sorrow.

—CHINESE PROVERB

Though patience be a tired mare,
  yet she will plod.

—SHAKESPEARE

Do not use a hatchet to remove a fly
  from your friend's forehead.

—CHINESE PROVERB

Distrust all in whom
  the impulse to punish is powerful.

—NIETZSCHE

Amongst all other vices there
  is none I hate more than cruelty,
  both by nature and judgement,
  as the extremest of all vices.

—MONTAIGNE

When in doubt,
  lean to the side of mercy.

—CERVANTES

The only moral lesson which is suited
  for a child — the most important
  lesson for every time of life — is this:
  Never hurt anybody.

—JEAN JACQUES ROUSSEAU

It is better to receive
  than to inflict an injury.

—CICERO

A blow in cold blood neither can
  nor should be forgiven.

—GEORGE BERNARD SHAW

All sins are attempts to fill voids.

—SIMONE WEIL

Rule your passions
  or they will rule you.

—HORACE

A man who has not passed through
  the inferno of his passions
  has never overcome them.

—CARL G. JUNG

Experience is a muffled lantern
  that throws light only on the bearer.

—CÉLINE

What is allowed, we scorn;
  what's not allowed, we burn for.

—OVID

The most malignant of thine enemies
  is the lust which abides within thee.

—SAADI

Delight of lust is gross and brief
And weariness treads on desire.

—PETRONIUS ARBITER

Not joy but joylessness
  is the mother of debauchery.

—NIETZSCHE

We should correct our own faults
  by seeing how uncomely
  they appear in others.

—FRANCIS BEAUMONT

Men's natures are alike; it is their habits
  that carry them far apart.

—CONFUCIUS

It seems, in fact, as though the
second half of a man's life is
made up of nothing but the habits he
has accumulated during the first half.

—DOSTOYEVSKY

A man's nature runs either to herbs, or
to weeds; therefore let him seasonably
water the one and destroy the other.

—SIR FRANCIS BACON

Let us not complain against men
because of their rudeness, their
ingratitude, their arrogance, their love
of self, their forgetfulness of others.
They are so made. Such is their
nature. To be annoyed with them is
like denouncing a stone for falling,
or a fire for burning.

—JEAN DE LA BRUYÈRE

The greatest mistake you can
make in life is to be continually
fearing you will make one.

—ELBERT G. HUBBARD

To make no mistakes is not in the
power of man, but from their errors
and mistakes the wise and the good
learn wisdom for the future.

—PLUTARCH

Fear is the mark of a slave.

—DIOGENES

Of all base passions,
fear is most acurs'd.

—SHAKESPEARE

A coward is always in danger.

—PORTUGUESE PROVERB

Guilt has very quick ears
to an accusation.

—HENRY FIELDING

The guilty flee where no one pursues.

—GREEK PROVERB

Shame is the mark of a base man,
and belongs to a character
capable of shameful acts.

—ARISTOTLE

Guilt is squalid.

—ELIZABETH BOWEN

Let other pens dwell on guilt
and misery. I quit such odious
subjects as soon as I can.

—JANE AUSTEN

It is the disposition of the thought
that altereth the nature of the thing.

—JOHN LYLY

Men are tormented by the
opinions they have of things,
not by the things themselves.

—GREEK PROVERB

There is only one real failure in life
that is possible, and that is,
not to be true to the best one knows.

—FREDERICK W. FARRAR

We lie loudest when
we lie to ourselves.

—ERIC HOFFER

Be so true to thyself
as thou be not false to others.

—SIR FRANCIS BACON

Honesty is the first chapter
in the book of wisdom.

—THOMAS JEFFERSON

Nature never deceives us;
it is always we who deceive ourselves.

—JEAN JACQUES ROUSSEAU

We never deceive for a
good purpose. Knavery always
adds malice to falsehood.

—JEAN DE LA BRUYÈRE

Malice drinks one half
of its own poison.

—SENECA

Sin has many tools, but a lie
is the handle that fits them all.

—OLIVER WENDELL HOLMES

Do not trust everybody.

—PITTACUS

You'll always have to deal with
bastards, being lied to, deceived,
slandered and ridiculed, but that's to
be expected and you must thank
heaven when you meet the exception.

—GUSTAVE FLAUBERT

In many ways the saying
 "Know thyself" is not well said.
 It were more practical to say
 "Know other people."

—MENANDER

The veriest nobodies
 are the greatest busybodies.

—BENJAMIN WHICHCOTE

Those who are fond of setting things
 right have no great objection
 to seeing them wrong.

—WILLIAM HAZLITT

Tale-bearers are as bad as tale-makers.

—RICHARD BRINSLEY SHERIDAN

A truth that's told with bad intent
 beats all the lies you can invent.

—WILLIAM BLAKE

The truth is often a terrible weapon
 of aggression. It is possible to lie,
 and even to murder, with the truth.

—ALFRED ADLER

Great damage is usually caused
 by those too scrupulous
 to do small harm.

—CARDINAL DE RETZ

Insensitive stupidity
 is the root of all the other vices.

—ALDOUS HUXLEY

Beware of a friend who
 has once been your enemy.

—FRENCH PROVERB

Of all the evil spirits
 abroad in the world,
 insincerity is the most dangerous.

—JAMES A. FROUDE

Pretending to be something you are not
 can lead to disaster.

—AESOP

One deceit produces another.

—TERENCE

If a person has no delicacy,
 he has you in his power.

—WILLIAM HAZLITT

Sloth rots the intelligence,
  cowardice destroys all power at the
  source, while vanity inhibits us from
  facing the facts which might teach us
  something; it dulls all other sensation.

—CYRIL CONNOLLY

That is true wisdom, to know
  how to alter one's mind
  when the occasion demands it.

—TERENCE

A man should never be ashamed
  to own he has been in the
  wrong, which is but saying,
  in other words, that he is wiser today
  than he was yesterday.

—ALEXANDER POPE

Jealousy is the greatest of all evils, and
  the least pitied by those who cause it.

—LA ROCHEFOUCAULD

Nothing on earth consumes a man
  more than the passion of resentment.

—NIETZSCHE

To jealousy, nothing is more frightful
  than laughter.

—FRANÇOISE SAGAN

A man that studieth revenge
  keepeth his own wounds green, which
  otherwise would heal and do well.

—SIR FRANCIS BACON

Jealousy is the apprehension
  of superiority.

—WILLIAM SHENSTONE

Never does the human soul
  appear so strong as when
  it forgoes revenge, and dares
  to forgive an injury.

—E. H. CHAPIN

There is more self-love
  than love in jealousy.

—LA ROCHFOUCAULD

Self-love, my liege, is not
  so vile a sin as self-neglecting.

—SHAKESPEARE

Revenge is ever the pleasure
  of a paltry spirit.

—LATIN PROVERB

Sloth ever finds justification.

—SEBASTIAN BRANT

Revenge, at first though sweet,
  bitter ere long back on itself recoils.

—JOHN MILTON

Life appears to me too short
to be spent nursing animosity
or registering wrong.

—CHARLOTTE BRONTË

To forget a wrong is the best revenge.

—ITALIAN PROVERB

Life cannot go on
without a great deal of forgetting.

—HONORÉ DE BALZAC

To be wronged is nothing,
unless you continue to remember it.

—CONFUCIUS

Memories make life beautiful,
forgetfulness alone makes it possible.

—ENRICO CIALDINI

You may be deceived if you trust too
much, but you will live in torment
if you do not trust enough.

—FRANK CRANE

Love all, trust a few, do wrong to none.

—SHAKESPEARE

Three things in human life are
important. The first is to be kind.
The second is to be kind.
And the third is to be kind.

—HENRY JAMES

Want of tenderness is want of parts,
and is no less a proof of stupidity
than depravity.

—SAMUEL JOHNSON

When you receive a kindness,
remember it; when you do a kindness,
forget it.

—GREEK PROVERB

Kindness in words creates confidence.
Kindness in thinking creates
profoundness. Kindness in giving
creates love.

—LAO-TSE

Autumn

SEPTEMBER

For each ecstatic instant
We must an anguish pay
In keen and quivering ratio
To the ecstasy.

—EMILY DICKINSON

INE wine is a triumph of perfect balance, wherein all elements combine in precisely the right proportion to produce a quality known to connoisseurs as *breed*. French vineyards have created fine wines since the dawn of the Christian era, and the artist illustrating the French Book of Days would most naturally choose the gathering and treading of grapes to signify the vintage month of September.

September, from the Latin *septem* or seven, was the seventh month of the primitive Roman year, which began in March. A shift of New Year's Day to January 1 has for centuries failed to make any difference as far as the name is concerned and what is actually the year's ninth month remains in name the seventh.

Mercury and a bountiful Virgo yield to Venus and Libra, the only inanimate figure in the zodiac circle of animals. Arriving as it does on the autumnal equinox, Libra, a Latin word meaning the Balance or Scales, makes perfect astrological sense, because once again day and night are of equal length.

Maintaining balance in a whirling world of time and chance is ever a challenge but one for which the sages can offer suggestions.

All things come into being by conflict
of opposites, and the sum of things
flows like a stream.

—HERACLITUS

Misfortune, wandering the same track
lights now upon one and now
upon another.

—AESCHYLUS

Blessings never come in pairs;
misfortunes never come alone.

—CHINESE PROVERB

All human acts involve more chance
than decision.

—ANDRÉ GIDE

Events do not come, they are there and
we encounter them on our way.

—ARTHUR STANLEY EDDINGTON

Ask not that events should happen
as you will, but let your will be that
events should happen as they do,
and you shall have peace.

—EPICTETUS

There is an ambush everywhere from
the army of accidents; therefore the
rider of life runs with loosened reins.

—HAFIZ

It is no wonder that chance has so
much power over us, since we live by
chance.

—SENECA

Chaos often breeds life,
when order breeds habit.

—HENRY ADAMS

Everything is sweetened by risk.

—ALEXANDER SMITH

The desire for safety stands against
every great and noble enterprise.

—TACITUS

Don't play for safety. It's the most
dangerous thing in the world.

—HUGH WALPOLE

The way to be safe is never to be
secure.

—BENJAMIN FRANKLIN

Monotony is the awful reward of the
careful.

—A. G. BUCKHAM

Security is mortal's chiefest enemy.

—ELLEN TERRY

During the first period
of a man's life the greatest danger
is not to take the risk.

—KIERKEGAARD

When there is no peril in the fight,
there is no glory in the triumph.

—CORNEILLE

Nothing happens to anybody which
he is not fitted by nature to bear.

—MARCUS AURELIUS

Misfortune is the test of a man's merit.

—SENECA

He has seen but half of the universe
who never has been shown
the house of pain.

—EMERSON

Sufferings are lessons.

—AESOP

We all have sufficient fortitude
to bear other people's misfortunes.

—LA ROCHEFOUCAULD

He who has a why to live
can bear almost any how.

—NIETZSCHE

Nothing is certain to man.

—OVID

The art of living is more like
that of wrestling than of dancing;
the main thing is to stand firm
and be ready for an unforeseen attack.

—MARCUS AURELIUS

Man is a pliable animal, a being who
gets accustomed to everything.

—DOSTOYEVSKY

Necessity is a powerful weapon.

—SENECA

Ability and necessity dwell
near each other.

—PYTHAGORAS

What is necessary is never a risk.

—CARDINAL DE RETZ

Nothing is hopeless,
we must hope for everything.

—EURIPIDES

Hope is a good breakfast,
but it is a bad supper.

—SIR FRANCIS BACON

In difficult situations when hope
seems feeble, the boldest plans are
safest.

—LIVY

You know the rule:
If you are falling, dive.

—JOSEPH CAMPBELL

Being mortal you must be prepared
for anything that might happen.

—XENOPHON

If you fell down yesterday,
stand up today.

—H. G. WELLS

A high heart ought to bear calamities
and not flee them, since in bearing
them appears the grandeur of
the mind and in fleeing them
the cowardice of the heart.

—PIETRO ARETINO

Experience is not what happens
to a man. It is what a man does
with what happens to him.

—ALDOUS HUXLEY

Self-pity is essentially humorless,
devoid of that lightness of touch
which gives understanding of life.

—ANTHONY POWELL

One ceases to be a child when
one realizes that telling one's troubles
does not make it any better.

—CESARE PAVESE

Those who do not complain
are never pitied.

—JANE AUSTEN

To hear complaints is wearisome alike
to the wretched and the happy.

—SAMUEL JOHNSON

Never complain and never explain.

—DISRAELI

It is equally futile and harmful to
complain to ourselves as to the
world.

—CESARE PAVESE

I never saw a wild thing sorry
for itself.

—D. H. LAWRENCE

Hide your misfortunes lest your
enemies rejoice.

—PERIANDER

All our misfortunes come
from not being able to be alone.

—JEAN DE LA BRUYÈRE

To be adult is to be alone.

—JEAN ROSTAND

By all means use sometimes to be
alone.

—GEORGE HERBERT

The greatest thing in the world
is to know how to be sufficient
unto oneself.

—MONTAIGNE

I was never less alone
than while by myself.

—EDWARD GIBBON

Get away from the crowd
when you can. Keep to yourself,
if only for a few hours daily.

—ARTHUR BRISBANE

If you are idle, be not solitary;
if you are solitary, be not idle.

—SAMUEL JOHNSON

In idleness there is perpetual despair.

—THOMAS CARLYLE

A life spent making mistakes is not
only more honorable but more
useful than a life spent doing
nothing.

—GEORGE BERNARD SHAW

Thanks to work we avoid three great
evils — boredom, vice and need.

—VOLTAIRE

Ennui has made more gamblers
than avarice, more drunkards
than thirst, and perhaps as many
suicides as despair.

—CHARLES CALEB COLTON

He who lives without folly
is not so wise as he imagines.

—LA ROCHEFOUCAULD

The mind ought sometimes to
be amused, that it may the better
return to thought, and to itself.

—PHAEDRUS

Look for the ridiculous in everything
and you will find it.

—JULES RENARD

Let not your tongue outrun your
  thought.

—CHILON

Loquacity has many pitfalls,
  silence none.

—APOLLONIUS OF TYANA

The reason why we have two ears
  and one mouth is that we may
  listen the more and talk the less.

—ZENO

Silence is not always tact and it is tact
  that is golden, not silence.

—SAMUEL BUTLER

Tact is the ability to describe others
  as they see themselves.

—ABRAHAM LINCOLN

Virtue is doing nothing to excess.

—SOCRATES

There is naught more beneficial
  than silence.

—MENANDER

Men fear silence as they fear solitude,
  because both give them a glimpse
  of the terror of life's nothingness.

—ANDRÈ MAUROIS

In the small hours, the emptiness of
  life seems more terrible than its
  misery.

—CYRIL CONNOLLY

The thought of suicide is a great
  consolation; with its help you
  can get through many a bad night.

—NIETZSCHE

You may not know it, but at the end
  of despair, there is a white clearing
  where one is almost happy.

—JEAN ANOUILH

Remember when life's path is steep
  to keep your mind even.

—HORACE

Suffering itself does less afflict
  the senses than the anticipation
  of suffering.

—QUINTILIAN

Imaginary evils soon become real ones
  by indulging our reflections on
  them.

—JONATHAN SWIFT

How much pain have cost us the evils
  which have never happened.

—THOMAS JEFFERSON

There are three motives to injurious
acts among men — hatred, envy,
and contempt; and these the wise man
overcomes by reason.

—EPICURUS

He who will not reason is a bigot;
he who cannot is a fool; and he
who dares not, is a slave.

—LORD BYRON

The habit of doing one's duty
drives away fear.

—CHARLES BAUDELAIRE

No courage is so great as that
which is born of utter desperation.

—SENECA

There is no education like adversity.

—DISRAELI

Self-trust is the essence of heroism.

—EMERSON

Moderation is the basis of morality
and man's most important virtue.

—NAPOLEON I

The most important thing in life is
never to have too much of anything.

—TERENCE

Enough is better than too much.

—FRENCH PROVERB

'Tis the wisest plan quickly to let go
that which we cannot hold.

—GIOVANNI GUARINI

Learn how to refuse favors.
This is a great and very useful art.

—THOMAS FULLER

I have always done myself
much harm by despising those people
for whom I have no respect.

—MONTESQUIEU

I have never met a man so ignorant
that I couldn't learn something
from him.

—GALILEO

To cultivate kindness is a valuable part
of the business of life.

—SAMUEL JOHNSON

The happiness of life consists
in being well-deceived.

—JONATHAN SWIFT

We believe we can change things
according to our wishes because
that's the only happy solution
we can see. We don't think of what
usually happens and what is also a
happy solution; things don't change,
but by and by our wishes change.

—MARCEL PROUST

Man was made for joy and woe;
And when this we rightly know,
Thro' the world we safely go.

—WILLIAM BLAKE

Advancing time sifts
and cleanses all alike.

—AESCHYLUS

Patience is a remedy for every sorrow.

—PUBLILIUS SYRUS

Never give up.

—HORACE

Patience is the key to all things.

—PERSIAN PROVERB

Life is not a spectacle or a feast;
it is a predicament.

—GEORGE SANTAYANA

For mortals, mortal things.
And all things leave us. Or if
they do not, then we leave them.

—LUCIAN

Every man on the foundations of his
own sufferings and joys, builds
for all.

—ALBERT CAMUS

What do we live for if it is not to
make life less difficult to each other?

—GEORGE ELIOT

Enjoy and give enjoyment, without
injury to thyself or to others: this is
true morality.

—NICOLAS CHAMFORT

A cheerful mind is a vigorous mind.

—NINON DE L'ENCLOS

The best of healers is good cheer.

—PINDAR

Comedy is the fountain of sound
sense.

—GEORGE MEREDITH

The most completely lost of all days
is the one on which we have
not laughed.

—NICOLAS CHAMFORT

A good laugh is sunshine in a house.

—WILLIAM THACKARAY

Laugh if you are wise.

—MARTIAL

Mirth is like a flash of lightning,
that breaks through a gloom of
clouds, and glitters for a moment;
cheerfulness keeps up a kind of
daylight in the mind, and fills it with
a steady and perpetual serenity.

—JOSEPH ADDISON

A perverse and fretful disposition
makes any state of life unhappy.

—CICERO

The highest wisdom is continual
cheerfulness; such a state,
like the region above the moon,
is always clear and serene.

—MONTAIGNE

The burden becomes light
when cheerfully borne.

—OVID

Austerity is a disease. I would
a thousand times rather be stricken
with fever than think gloomily.

—VOLTAIRE

All of us must indulge
in a few small follies if we
are to make reality bearable.

—MARCEL PROUST

The one serious conviction
that a man should have is that
nothing is to be taken too seriously.

—SAMUEL BUTLER

The more seriously one takes
an amusement, the more amusing
it becomes.

—A. C. BENSON

Humankind cannot bear
very much reality.

—T. S. ELIOT

We have in ourselves, without
being able to know why, wherefore
or whence, the need to deceive
ourselves constantly by creating a
reality (one for each and never the
same for all), which from time to
time is discovered to be vain and
illusory.

—LUIGI PIRANDELLO

The world is an illusion, but an
illusion which we must
take seriously.

—ALDOUS HUXLEY

Society must have faith in its illusions
and yet paradoxically remember
they are illusions. It must have
its mythology, like the Greeks;
and live by its myths.

—HENRY JAMES

There's only one success — to be able
to spend your life in your own way.

—CHRISTOPHER MORLEY

You have to keep open and
aware directly to the urges that
motivate you. Keep the channel open.

—MARTHA GRAHAM

As leaves on trees,
such is the life of man.

—PYRRHO

The world is wide; not two days are
alike, nor even two hours; neither
was there ever two leaves of a tree
alike since the creation of the world.

—JOHN CONSTABLE

The most universal quality is diversity.

—MONTAIGNE

What a man is worth is
so much what he becomes.

—ANTOINE DE SAINT-EXUPERY

Probe the earth and see where
your main roots run.

—THOREAU

Truth is never pure, and rarely simple.

—OSCAR WILDE

Truth, like light, is dazzling. By
contrast, untruth is a beautiful
sunset that enhances everything.

—ALBERT CAMUS

Nothing creates such untruth
as the wish to please or
to be spared something.

—SHIRLEY HAZZARD

Don't be too anxious to please.

—MARTIAL

Do not confuse the pleasure of
pleasing with the happiness of
loving.

—COCO CHANEL

He who tries to please everybody
pleases nobody.

—AESOP

The art of pleasing consists
in being pleased.

—WILLIAM HAZLITT

There is no cure for birth and death
save to enjoy the interval.

—GEORGE SANTAYANA

Laugh and be well.

—MATTHEW GREEN

Only the paradox comes anywhere near
to comprehending the fullness of life.

—CARL G. JUNG

There is only one truth, steadfast,
healing, salutary, and that is
the absurd.

—ANDREW SALMON

Why shouldn't things be largely
absurd, futile, and transitory?
They are so, and we are so,
and they and we go very well
together.

—GEORGE SANTAYANA

Good actions enoble us, and
we are the sons of our own deeds.

—CERVANTES

Know how to bear the changes
of fortune with nobility.

—CLEOBULUS

Wisdom denotes the pursuing
of the best ends by the best means.

—FRANCIS HUTCHESON

Autumn

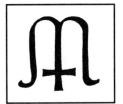

OCTOBER

Don't walk in front of me — I may not follow,
Don't walk behind me — I may not lead.
Walk beside me — and just be my friend.

—ALBERT CAMUS

THE eighth month of the old Roman calendar marks the height of autumn, a season of ripeness and decay. There's a chill in the air, for the crisis of winter is at hand and all living creatures must strive to meet the challenge and survive.

The artist depicts a near-frenzy of farm activity in accord with the ever shorter days and diminishing light. Livestock are brought in to shelter, their feed threshed and stored. Fields are plowed and sown with winter grain — not only as a crop but as a blanket to protect the soil from winter's icy grasp. Hungry birds threaten the enterprise.

Even the zodiac inset of Libra indicates a certain sense of apprehension. The scales are held in only tentative balance by a female figure, possibly the star-maiden Astraea who in medieval allegory personified justice. Her departure from Earth coincided with the ending of Saturn's reign — a mythical Golden Age. The sun enters the dark sign of the Scorpion as the month ends and planetary rulership passes from an uneasy Venus to the formidable Mars.

The time is ripe now to consider our species' place in the universal pattern, our duty to nature's forces, to one another, and to ourselves. It behooves us to examine and to recognize the inherent kinship existing among the animal, vegetable and mineral kingdoms of our planet.

It is wise to harken, not to me,
  but to my word, and to confess
  that all things are one.

—HERACLITUS

The earth does not belong to us;
  we belong to the earth. All things
  are connected like the blood which
  unites one family.

—CHIEF SEATTLE

That which is above is like that
  which is below, to perpetuate
  the miracle of one thing.

—HERMES TRISMEGISTUS

We're not at one. We've no instinctive
  knowledge like migratory birds.

—RILKE

It is a false dichotomy to think
  of nature and man. Mankind
  is that factor in nature which
  exhibits in its most intense form
  the plasticity of nature.

—ALFRED NORTH WHITEHEAD

Man has lost the capacity to foresee
  and to forestall. He will end
  by destroying the earth.

—ALBERT SCHWEITZER

Adapt or perish, now as ever,
  is Nature's inexorable imperature.

—H. G. WELLS

It takes time to ruin a world,
  but time is all it takes.

—BERNARD DE FONTENELLE

In wildness is the preservation
of the world.

—THOREAU

The wild places are where we began.
When they end, so do we.

—DAVID BROWER

There is no spot of ground, however
arid, bare, or ugly, that cannot be
tamed into such a state as may give
the impression of beauty and delight.

—GERTRUDE JEKYLL

You become responsible, forever,
for what you have tamed.

—ANTOINE DE SAINT-EXUPÉRY

Nature, to be commanded,
must be obeyed.

—SIR FRANCIS BACON

That man can interrogate as well
as observe nature was a lesson
slowly learned in his evolution.

—SIR WILLIAM OSLER

The path of duty lies in the
thing that is nearby, but
men seek it in things far off.

—CHINESE PROVERB

Our grand business is undoubtedly not
to see what lies dimly at a distance,
but to do what lies clearly at hand.

—THOMAS CARLYLE

Beware while you are guarding the
sky, you lose the earth.

—VALERIUS MAXIMUS

I slept and dreamed that life
was beauty. I woke — and found
that life was duty.

—ELLEN STURGIS HOOPER

There are only three absolute
virtues: objectivity, courage,
and a sense of responsibility.

—ARTHUR SCHNITZLER

The ability to accept responsibility
is the measure of man.

—ROY L. SMITH

Ability involves responsibility;
power to its last particle is duty.

—IAN McLAREN

Knowest thou not, that thou canst
not move a step on this earth without
finding some duty to be done, and that
every man is useful to his kind
by the very fact of his existence?

—THOMAS CARLYLE

There is not a moment
without some duty.

—CICERO

Do not plan for ventures
before finishing what is at hand.

—EURIPIDES

Nothing is more dangerous
than discontinued labor: it is
habit lost. A habit easy to abandon,
difficult to resume.

—VICTOR HUGO

Every duty that is bidden to wait
comes back with seven fresh duties
at its back.

—CHARLES KINGSLEY

The reward of one duty done
is the power to fulfill another.

—GEORGE ELIOT

There is no growth except in
the fulfillment of obligations.

—ANTOINE DE SAINT-EXUPÉRY

Every system should allow
loopholes and exceptions, for
if it does not it will in the end
crush all that is best in man.

—BERTRAND RUSSELL

The one thing more difficult
than following a regimen is keeping
from imposing it on others.

—MARCEL PROUST

Adapt yourself to the things
among which your lot
has been cast and love
sincerely the fellow creatures
with whom destiny has ordained
that you shall live.

—MARCUS AURELIUS

What you cannot avoid, welcome.

—MONTENEGRIN PROVERB

We do not free ourselves from
something by avoiding it,
but only by living through it.

—CESARE PAVASE

Facing it — always facing it — that's
the way to get through. Face it!
That's enough for any man.

—JOSEPH CONRAD

Remember this, — that there is
a proper dignity and proportion
to be observed in the performance
of every act of life.

—MARCUS AURELIUS

Without work all life goes rotten.

—ALBERT CAMUS

There is no substitute for hard work.

—THOMAS A. EDISON

It is only well with me when
I have a chisel in my hand.

—MICHELANGELO

By means of work one
exceeds one's capacities.

—JULES RENARD

Happiness is activity

—ARISTOTLE

Labor itself is a pleasure.

—LATIN PROVERB

The fruit derived from labor
is the sweetest of all pleasures.

—VAUVENARGUES

Toil and pleasure, in their nature
opposites, are yet linked together in
a kind of necessary connection.

—LIVY

As a remedy against all ills — poverty,
sickness, and melancholy — only
one thing is absolutely necessary:
a liking for work.

—CHARLES BAUDELAIRE

No human pursuit achieves dignity
until it can be called work, and
when you can experience a physical
loneliness for the tools of your trade,
you can see that other things — the
experiments, the irrelevant vocations,
the vanities you used to hold — were
false to you.

—BERYL MARKHAM

All energy spent on conscious work
is an investment.

—G. I. GURDJIEFF

To get profit without risk, experience
without danger, and reward without
work, is as impossible as it is to live
without being born.

—A. P. GOUTHEY

I don't like work — no man does — but
I like what is in work — the chance
to find yourself.

—JOSEPH CONRAD

All happiness depends on courage
and work. I have had many periods
of wretchedness, but with energy,
and above all, with illusions,
I pulled through them all.

—HONORÉ DE BALZAC

Nothing is really work unless you'd
rather be doing something else.

—JAMES M. BARRIE

Work is much more fun than fun.

—NOËL COWARD

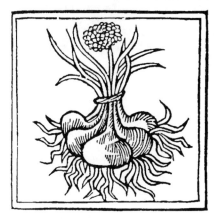

We work not only to produce
but to give value to time.

—EUGÈNE DELACROIX

Time is the great comforter of grief,
but the agency by which it works
is exhaustion.

—LETITIA ELIZABETH LANDON

Sorrow's best antidote is employment.

—EDWARD YOUNG

We do not choose our own parts
in life and have nothing to do with
those parts. Our duty is confined
to playing them well.

—EPICTETUS

Who does the best his circumstances
allow does well, acts nobly;
angels could do no more.

—EDWARD YOUNG

Do your duty until it
becomes your joy.

—MARIE VON EBNER-ESCHENBACH

Live all you can; it's a mistake not to.
It doesn't matter what you do
in particular, so long as you have
your life. If you haven't had that
what have you had?

—HENRY JAMES

Most of all reverence thyself.

—LATIN PROVERB

Conduct is three-fourths of your life
and its largest concern.

—MATTHEW ARNOLD

Never esteem anything as
of advantage to thee that shall
make thee break thy word
or lose thy self-respect.

—MARCUS AURELIUS

Everything without tells the
individual that he is nothing;
everything within persuades him
that he is everything.

—XAVIER DOUDAN

So much is the man worth
as he esteems himself.

—RABELAIS

If you wish success in life, make
perseverance your bosom friend,
experience your wise counsellor,
caution your elder brother
and hope your guardian angel.

—JOSEPH ADDISON

No one has any right save that
of always doing his duty.

—AUGUSTE COMTE

A sense of duty is useful in work,
but offensive in personal relations.

—BERTRAND RUSSELL

The anger of an enemy represents
our faults or admonishes us of our
duty with more heartiness than
the kindness of a friend.

—JEREMY TAYLOR

Pay attention to your enemies,
for they are the first to discover
your mistakes.

—ANTISTHENES

One's own self is well hidden
from one's own self: of all mines
of treasure, one's own is the last
to be dug up.

—NIETZSCHE

It many times falls out that we deem
ourselves much deceived in others,
because we first deceived ourselves.

—SIR PHILIP SIDNEY

Nothing is so easy as to deceive
oneself; for each man readily believes
what he wishes to be true, even though
the truth is far otherwise.

—DEMOSTHENES

The mind is always prone to
believe what it wishes to be true.

—HELIODORUS

To understand oneself is the classic
form of consolation; to elude oneself
is the romantic.

—GEORGE SANTAYANA

Every man, however wise, needs
the advice of some sagacious friend
in the affairs of life.

—PLAUTUS

Things that have a common quality
  ever quickly seek their kind.

—MARCUS AURELIUS

True friendship can only spring
  from perfect sympathy.

—SALLUST

Friendship either finds or makes
  equals.

—PUBLILIUS SYRUS

Friends are born, not made.

—HENRY ADAMS

When a friend asks,
  there is no tomorrow.

—ENGLISH PROVERB

Ne're shall I, while in my senses,
  ever think any blessing equal to that
  of an agreeable true friend.

—HORACE

Hold a true friendship
  with both your hands.

—NIGERIAN PROVERB

Friends do not live in harmony
  merely, as some say, but in melody.

—THOREAU

Friendship should be surrounded
  with ceremonies and respects,
  and not crushed into corners.

—EMERSON

Be a friend to thyself,
  and others will befriend thee.

—ENGLISH PROVERB

One's friends are that part
  of the human race with whom
  one can be human.

—GEORGE SANTAYANA

In giving advice seek to help,
  not to please, your friend.

—SOLON

Only those who have helped
  themselves know how to help others,
  and to respect their right
  to help themselves.

—GEORGE BERNARD SHAW

It is not so much our friends' help
  that helps us as the confidence
  of their help.

—EPICURUS

No power can defend or sanction
  treachery against a friend.

—OVID

To take refuge with an inferior
is to betray one's self.

—PUBLILIUS SYRUS

There is an unfortunate
disposition in man to attend
much more to the faults of his
companions that offend him, than to
their perfections that please him.

—SIR FULKE GREVILLE

In managing human affairs, there
is no better rule than self-restraint.

—LAO-TSE

A man who does not trust himself,
never truly trusts anyone.

—CARDINAL DE RETZ

What loneliness is more lonely
than distrust?

—GEORGE ELIOT

One must be fond of people
and trust them if one is not
to make a mess of life.

—E. M. FORSTER

It is more shameful to mistrust your
friends than to be deceived by them.

—LA ROCHEFOUCAULD

Think on this doctrine, — that
reasoning beings were created for
one another's sake; that to be patient
is a branch of justice, and that men
sin without intending it.

—MARCUS AURELIUS

He that cannot forgive others breaks
the bridge over which he must pass
himself; for every man has need
to be forgiven.

—THOMAS FULLER

Treat people as if they were
what they ought to be and you
help them to become what
they are capable of being.

—GOETHE

He removes the greatest ornament
of friendship, who takes away
from it respect.

—CICERO

Friendship is like earthenware, once
broken it can be mended; love is like
a mirror, once broken that ends it.

—JOSH BILLINGS

At best, the renewal of broken
relations is a nervous matter.

—HENRY ADAMS

If you would have friends,
first learn to do without them.

—ELBERT G. HUBBARD

Happiness belongs to the
self-sufficient.

—ARISTOTLE

As long as a man is capable of
self-renewal he is a living being.

—HENRI FRÉDÉRIC AMIEL

Consciousness of our powers
increases them.

—VAUVENARGUES

The earth teaches us more about
ourselves than all the books.
Because it resists us. Man discovers
himself when he measures himself
against the obstacle.

—ANTOINE DE SAINT-EXUPÉRY

Nature, in her indifference, makes
no distinction between good and evil.

—ANATOLE FRANCE

They have a right to censure,
that have a heart to help:
the rest is cruelty, not justice.

—WILLIAM PENN

Justice consists in doing no injury
to men; decency in giving them
no offense.

—CICERO

I think the first duty
of society is justice.

—ALEXANDER HAMILTON

When a man wants to murder a tiger,
he calls it sport: when the tiger wants
to murder him, he calls it ferocity.
The distinction between crime
and justice is no greater.

—GEORGE BERNARD SHAW

There is a certain respect, a general
duty of humanity, that attaches us
not only to animals who have life
and feeling, but even to trees and
plants.

—MONTAIGNE

Nature is a labyrinth in which the
very haste you move with will
make you lose your way.

—SIR FRANCIS BACON

What is man without the beasts?
  If all the beasts were gone, man
  would die from great loneliness of
  spirit, for whatever happens
  to the beasts also happens to man.

—CHIEF SEATTLE

When a man has pity on all living
  creatures then only is he noble.

—BUDDHA

A creature in distress
  is a sacred object.

—OVID

It is sacred even to love a dog.
  And we have the right — as sacred
  as life itself — not to have to
  justify it to anyone.

—MARGUERITE DURAS

Virtue debases itself
  by justifying itself.

—VOLTAIRE

If you really understand an
  animal so that he gets to trust you
  completely and, within his limits,
  understands you, there grows
  up between you affection of a
  purity and simplicity which seems to
  me peculiarly satisfactory.

—LEONARD WOOLF

Histories are more full of examples of
  the fidelity of dogs than of friends.

—ALEXANDER POPE

There is no secret so close as that
  between a rider and his horse.

—R. S. SURTEES

Animals are such agreeable
  friends — they ask no questions,
  they pass no criticisms.

—GEORGE ELIOT

When I play with my cat, who
  knows but that she regards me
  more as a plaything than I do her?

—MONTAIGNE

What's wonderful in the animal world
  is the way they know everything
  without telling each other... and far
  away! at the speed of light.

—CÉLINE

The world of the living contains
  enough marvels and mysteries acting
  upon our emotions and intelligence
  in ways so inexplicable that it would
  almost justify the conception of life
  as an enchanted state.

—JOSEPH CONRAD

Autumn

NOVEMBER

The woods are lovely, dark and deep.
But I have promises to keep,
And miles to go before I sleep,
And miles to go before I sleep.

—ROBERT FROST

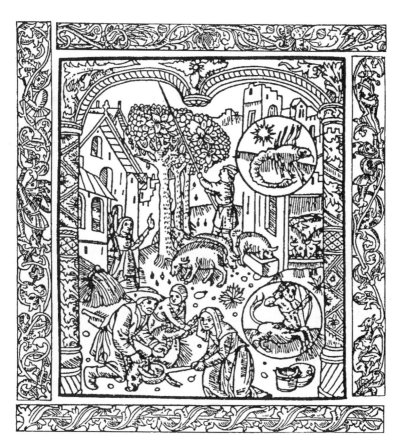

DEATH is the melancholy theme of autumn's final month. The Saxon tribes called November *Blot-monath*, blood month, for it was slaughter time when beasts were slain, drained of blood, and salted for winter provisions. Many Books of Days picture this grim practice as emblematic of the ninth month.

Our French woodcut is no exception. In the foreground, a pig is jugulated and its blood collected to make culinary treats. In the background, a man uses a pole to shake down nuts from the tree for fattening the pigs. Oblivious of their fate, the swine feast in an enclosure and forage outside on their own. A woman bearing torches emerges from a doorway. Is she a folk memory of the classical goddesses of the underworld who were often portrayed carrying lighted torches? Or could this be a pictorial comment on the increasing darkness overtaking the world?

One cheerful note is the appearance of the jovial Archer of Sagittarius, a harbinger of change, light, and hope.

November is the time of year to contemplate the more negative aspects of life's reality: pain, loss, old age, judgement and death itself.

Death is the cooling night,
and life the sultry day.

—HEINRICH HEINE

The gods conceal from men the
happiness of death, that they
may endure life.

—LUCAN

Suns may rise and set; we, when our
short day has closed, must sleep on
during one perpetual night.

—CATULLUS

Life may be considered altogether
as a dream, and death as the
awakening from sleep.

—SCHOPENHAUER

Every exit is an entry somewhere else.

—TOM STOPPARD

We don't know life:
how can we know death?

—CONFUCIUS

The nearer I approach death the more
I feel like one who is in sight of land
at last and is about to anchor in his
home port after a long voyage.

—CICERO

Life is a voyage and death
its port of arrival.

—ANTONIO PEREZ

To die is landing
on some distant shore.

—JOHN DRYDEN

We must ask where we are
and whither we are tending.

—ABRAHAM LINCOLN

All men should strive to learn before
they die what they are running from,
and to, and why.

—JAMES THURBER

A man may by custom fortify himself
against pain, shame and suchlike
accidents; but as to death, we can
experience it but once, and we are all
apprentices when we come to it.

—MONTAIGNE

There are only three events in a
man's life: birth, life and death:
he is not conscious of being born,
he dies in pain, and he forgets to live.

—JEAN DE LA BRUYÈRE

The long habit of living
indisposeth us for dying.

—SIR THOMAS BROWNE

All that live must die.

—SHAKESPEARE

There await men after death
such things as they neither expect
nor have any conception of.

—HERACLITUS

Death is sometimes
a punishment, often a gift;
to many it has been a favor.

—SENECA

Death is a delightful hiding place
for weary men.

—HERODOTUS

Death is the golden key
that opens the palace of eternity.

—JOHN MILTON

The art of living is the art
of knowing how to believe lies.

     —CESARE PAVESE

I have a passion for truth, and
for the fictions that it authorizes.

     —JULES RENARD

'Tis strange — but true: for truth is
always strange; stranger than fiction.

     —LORD BYRON

Man is a poetical animal
and delights in fiction.

     —WILLIAM HAZLITT

Take the life-lie away from
the average man and straight away
you take away his happiness.

     —HENRIK IBSEN

I think on death as the apparent end
of the illusions that encompass us.
They all have a sudden and unexpected end, that challenges any faith
we have pinned to their worth.

     —VACHEL LINDSAY

As is the sense of sight in the body,
so is mind in the soul.

     —ARISTOTLE

The loss of illusions
is the death of the soul.

     —NICOLAS CHAMFORT

When I examine myself and my
methods of thought I come to the
conclusion that the gift of fantasy
has meant more to me than my talent
for absorbing knowledge.

     —ALBERT EINSTEIN

When someone says that those
people who feel the least are happiest,
I'm always reminded of the Hindu
proverb: Sitting is better than
standing, lying is better than sitting,
but the best thing of all is to be dead.

—NICOLAS CHAMFORT

Idle men are dead all their life long.

—THOMAS FULLER

Peace of mind and freedom
from pain are pleasures which imply
a state of rest; joy and delight
are present in motion and activity.

—EPICURUS

The most general survey shows us
that the two foes of human
happiness are pain and boredom.

—SCHOPENHAUER

Man is the only animal
that can be bored.

—ERICH FROMM

The happy people are those who
are producing something; the
bored people are consuming much
and producing nothing.

—DEAN INGE

Boredom is therefore a vital problem
for the moralist, since at least half
the sins of mankind are caused
by the fear of it.

—BERTRAND RUSSELL

Isn't life a hundred times too short
for us to bore ourselves?

—NIETZSCHE

Habit is the deepest
law of human nature.

          —THOMAS CARLYLE

Powerful indeed
is the empire of habit.

          —PUBLILIUS SYRUS

All habits gather, by unseen degrees, as
brooks make rivers, rivers run to seas.

          —JOHN DRYDEN

Habit is either the best of servants
or the worst of masters.

          —NATHANIEL EMMONS

I take it to be a principle
rule of life, not to be too much
addicted to any one thing.

          —TERENCE

Nothing is more powerful than habit.

          —OVID

The evolution from happiness to habit
is one of death's best weapons.

          —JULIO CORTAZAR

Habits form a second nature.

          —JEAN BAPTISTE LAMARK

The most unendurable thing, to be
sure, the really terrible thing, would
be a life without habits, a life which
continually required improvisation.

          —NIETZSCHE

Wise living consists less
in acquiring good habits than in
acquiring as few habits as possible.

          —ERIC HOFFER

To know how to grow old is
the masterwork of wisdom,
and one of the most difficult
chapters in the great art of living.

—HENRI FRÉDÉRIC AMIEL

Growing old is no more than
a bad habit which a busy man
has no time to learn.

—ANDRÉ MAUROIS

The older one gets, the larger
one's horizons. But the possibilities
of life get smaller and smaller.

—FRANZ KAFKA

Childhood goes by you like a
locomotive. Then your career rushes
by. But there are moments when
we're humiliated or enlightened
and by them forever changed.

—DOROTHY JEAKINS

There's no doubt that old age is a
journey into a foreign country,
so that one is constantly being
astonished by what is not possible.

—MAY SARTON

Not to be able to grow old
is just as ridiculous as to
be unable to outgrow childhood.

—CARL G. JUNG

I am certain there is no greater
misfortune than to have a heart
that will not grow old.

—DISRAELI

Old age most proclaims itself
when it tries hardest to hide itself.

—LUIS DE LEON

There is no greater error of age than
to suppose that it can recover the
enjoyment of youth by possessing
itself of what youth only can enjoy.

—SIR HENRY TAYLOR

This downhill path is easy,
but there's no turning back.

—CHRISTINA ROSSETTI

The longer one lives, the less
importance one attaches to
things, and also the less
importance to importance.

—JEAN ROSTAND

Youth, which is forgiven everything,
forgives itself nothing: age,
which forgives itself everything,
is forgiven nothing.

—GEORGE BERNARD SHAW

The world's a bubble; and
the life of man less than a span.

—SIR FRANCIS BACON

Anticipate change as though
you had left it behind you.

—RILKE

Age is a matter of feeling,
not of years.

—GEORGE W. CURTIS

We are always the same age inside.

—GERTRUDE STEIN

Anyone who keeps the ability
to see beauty never grows old.

—FRANZ KAFKA

Youth has only spring green tones;
we others of the more advanced
season, have a thousand shades,
one more beautiful than the other.

—COUNT DE BUSSY-RABUTIN

As we grow old the beauty
steals inward.

—EMERSON

There is nothing more beautiful
than cheerfulness in an old face.

—JEAN PAUL RICHTER

To grow old is to pass
from passion to compassion.

—ALBERT CAMUS

The gradually declining years are
among the sweetest in a man's life.

—SENECA

Life's evening will take its character
from the day that preceded it.

—PHILIP N. SHUTTLEWORTH

In old age we understand better
how to avert troubles; in youth,
how to endure them.

—SCHOPENHAUER

Being young is beautiful,
but being old is comfortable.

—MARIE VON EBNER-ESCHENBACH

It is always the season
for the old to learn.

—AESCHYLUS

There is nothing more remarkable
in the life of Socrates than that he
found time in his old age to learn
to dance and play on instruments,
and thought it was time well spent.

—MONTAIGNE

We are so used to disguising
our real selves from others,
that the disguise in the end,
deceives even us who wear it.

—LA ROCHEFOUCAULD

Man is least himself when he talks
in his own person. Give him a mask
and he will tell the truth.

—OSCAR WILDE

Nothing gives more assurance
than a mask.

—COLETTE

No mask like open truth to cover lies,
as to go naked is the best disguise.

—WILLIAM CONGREVE

A man's true worth can be measured
by considering the degree and the
manner in which he has succeeded
in liberating himself from his ego.

—ALBERT EINSTEIN

You can tell the character
of every man when you see
how he receives praise.

—SENECA

Great tranquillity of heart is his who
cares neither for praise nor blame.

—THOMAS À KEMPIS

One must judge men, not by
their opinions, but by what their
opinions have made of them.

—GEORG C. LICHTENBERG

You shall judge a man by his foes
as well as by his friends.

—JOSEPH CONRAD

Friends may come and go,
but enemies accumulate.

—THOMAS JONES

If you have no enemies,
it's a sign fortune has forgot you.

—THOMAS FULLER

He will never make true friends
who is afraid of making enemies.

—WILLIAM HAZLITT

All men's friend is all men's fool.

—FRISIAN PROVERB

In friends who have turned against us
we find our bitterest enemies.

—BALTASAR GRACIAN

It is easier to forgive an enemy
than to forgive a friend.

—WILLIAM BLAKE

Friendships begin with liking
or gratitude — roots that
can be pulled up.

—GEORGE ELIOT

Observe people when they are angry,
for it is then that their true nature
is revealed.

—THE ZOHAR

A fit of anger is as fatal to dignity
as a dose of arsenic is to life.

—JOSIAH G. HOLLAND

Nothing is more characteristic of a
man than the manner in which he
behaves toward fools.

—HENRI FRÉDÉRIC AMIEL

There is none can baffle men of sense
but fools, on whom they can make
no impression.

—WILLIAM SHENSTONE

Men show their characters
in nothing more clearly than
in what they think laughable.

—GOETHE

It is in trifles, and when he
is off guard, that a man
shows his character.

—SCHOPENHAUER

Always judge a person by
the way he treats someone
who can be of no use to him.

—ANONYMOUS

All men judge the acts
of others by what they
would have done themselves.

—DIONYSIUS

Don't wait for the Last Judgement.
It takes place every day.

—ALBERT CAMUS

Blessed is he who has learned
  to bear what he cannot change
  and to sacrifice with dignity
  what he cannot save.

                  —SCHILLER

Sorrow is that state of mind
  in which our desires are
  fixed upon the past without
  looking forward to the future.

           —SAMUEL JOHNSON

Everyone can master a grief
  but he that has it.

              —SHAKESPEARE

Maybe that's what we're looking
  for all through life, just this, the
  greatest possible sorrow so we
  can become ourselves before dying.

                  —CÉLINE

It is dangerous to abandon oneself
  to the luxury of grief: it deprives
  one of courage and even of
  the wish for recovery.

       —HENRI FRÉDÉRIC AMIEL

Melancholy is the pleasure
  of being sad.

             —VICTOR HUGO

Never give way to melancholy, resist it
  steadily, for the habit will encroach.

            —SYDNEY SMITH

The only cure for grief is action.

             —G.H. LEWES

Life begins on the
  other side of despair.

         —JEAN-PAUL SARTRE

Age and sorrow have the gift
  of reading the future by the past.

— FREDERICK W. FARRAR

The deep pain that is felt at the
  death of every friendly soul arises
  from the feeling that there is in
  every individual something which
  is inexpressible, peculiar to him
  alone and is therefore absolutely
  and irretrievably lost.

— SCHOPENHAUER

Happiness is good for the body
  but sorrow strengthens the spirit.

— MARCEL PROUST

If some persons died, and others
  did not die, death would
  indeed be a terrible affliction.

— JEAN DE LA BRUYÈRE

I not only bow to the inevitable;
  I am fortified by it.

— THORNTON WILDER

Certainly there are good and bad
  times, but our mood changes more
  often than our fortune.

— JULES RENARD

Life does not cease to be funny when
  people die anymore than it ceases to
  be serious when people laugh.

— GEORGE BERNARD SHAW

It is equally pointless to weep
  because we won't be alive a hundred
  years from now as that we were
  not here a hundred years ago.

— MONTAIGNE

Life is a jest; and all things show it.
  I thought so once; but now I know it.

— JOHN GAY

It is a modest creed, and yet pleasant
  if one considers it; to own
  that death itself must be like
  all the rest, a mockery.

— SHELLEY

Who hath not known ill fortune,
never knew himself or his virtue.

—DAVID MALLET

The optimist claims we live
in the best of all possible worlds.
The pessimist fears this is true.

—JAMES BRANCH CABELL

Pessimism, when you get used to it,
is just as agreeable as optimism.

—ARNOLD BENNETT

Nothing is miserable, unless you
think it so; conversely every lot
is happy if you are content with it.

—BOETHIUS

Observe always that everything
is the result of change, and get
used to thinking that there is
nothing Nature loves so well as
to change existing forms and
to make new ones like them.

—MARCUS AURELIUS

Sometimes the best gain is to lose.

—GEORGE HERBERT

The art of losing isn't hard to master;
so many things seem filled with
intent to be lost that their loss
is no disaster.

—ELIZABETH BISHOP

I have often observed that
resignation is never so perfect
as when the blessing denied
begins to lose somewhat of its
value in our eyes.

—JANE AUSTEN

Losses are comparative, imagination
only what makes them
of any moment.

—BLAISE PASCAL

The loss that is not known,
is no loss at all.

—PUBLILIUS SYRUS

Remember that no captain
ever makes port with all the cargo
with which he sets sail.

—HENRY JAMES

We are close to waking up when
we dream that we are dreaming.

—NOVALIS

There is no cure for birth and death
save to enjoy the interval.

—GEORGE SANTAYANA

Winter

DECEMBER

Hail to thee, blithe Spirit!
Bird thou never wert,
That from Heaven, or near it,
Pourest thy full heart
In profuse strains of unpremeditated art.

—SHELLEY

GLOOM settles over the earth as the sun visibly weakens, rising later and setting earlier with each passing day. Just when a cataclysm appears inevitable, the sun seems to stand still, turn and begin its return journey. From earliest times winter solstice — the longest night of the year — was an occasion for celebration with the last portion of December given over to feasting and merrymaking throughout Europe. In the north, Yuletide welcomed the return of the sun with decorated evergreens and joyful festivities. The Romans observed Saturnalia with a great banquet commemorating an idyllic era when all people were equal. Slaves were waited on by their masters and the wealthy gave gifts to the poor.

Pagan traditions live on hidden among Christmas customs.

Jupiter's fiery Centaur yields to Saturn's Goat of Capricorn. The Lady of the Manor oversees preparation of what may be the Christmas feast. The medieval kitchen is a scene of creative activity as the harvest grain ground to flour is moistened, kneaded and baked into bread. Individual casseroles of meat, legumes and herbs simmer in another oven. Certainly cuisine ranks high on the scale of human cultural achievements with the French having perfected the art of cookery.

Civilization was attained by way of agriculture and the arts — a worthy triumph of human imagination and creativity.

There's only one corner of the
  universe you can be certain of
  improving, and that's your own self.

—ALDOUS HUXLEY

The pattern of a creative life
  is to find a self, to express that self
  and to take the consequences.

—GARSON KANIN

The will which commands itself
  is the creative will. It makes a whole
  out of fragments and riddles of life.

—PAUL TILLICH

Man has been endowed with reason,
  with the power to create, so that
  he can add to what he's been given.

—ANTON CHEKHOV

The gods plant reason in mankind,
  of all good gifts the highest.

—SOPHOCLES

Enthusiasm is the fever of reason.

—VICTOR HUGO

Convictions are more dangerous
  enemies of truth than lies.

—NIETZSCHE

Nothing is so firmly believed
  as that of which we know least.

—MONTAIGNE

Happiness is not an ideal of reason
  but of imagination.

—IMMANUEL KANT

The world overcomes us, not merely
by appealing to our reason, or
by exciting our passions, but by
imposing on our imagination.

—CARDINAL JOHN NEWMAN

Imagination cannot make fools wise;
but she can make them happy,
to the envy of reason, who can
only make her friends miserable.

—BLAISE PASCAL

The imagination is in closer
accord with the understanding
than with the will.

—RAMON LULL

To try to understand is to never
understand. Either everything is
understood at once, by the heart,
or it is never understood at all.

—MERVYN PEAKE

Life is arduous, difficult, a perpetual
struggle. It calls for gigantic courage
and strength. More than anything,
perhaps, creatures of illusion as we
are, it calls for confidence in oneself.

—VIRGINIA WOOLF

When one has arrived at certainty,
he experiences one of the greatest
joys which the human heart can feel.

—LOUIS PASTEUR

I am certain of nothing but
the holiness of the heart's affections
and the truth of imagination — what
the imagination seizes as beauty must
be truth — whether it existed before
or not.

—JOHN KEATS

The imagination lives a life of its own.

—HENRY JAMES

Mankind is governed
  by its imagination.

—NAPOLEON I

We may affirm absolutely that
  nothing great in the world has been
  accomplished without passion.

—HEGEL

Truth can only be found by seeking it.

—PLATO

Most of the change we think we
  see in life is due to truths being
  in and out of favor.

—ROBERT FROST

Truth — what we think it is
  at any given moment of time.

—LUIGI PIRANDELLO

We have to live today by what truth
  we can get today and be ready
  tomorrow to call it falsehood.

—WILLIAM JAMES

Everything possible to be believed
  is an image of truth.

—WILLIAM BLAKE

If I had a fistful of truths,
  I would open it for no one.

—BERNARD DE FONTENELLE

Truth will sooner come out of error
  than from confusion.

—SIR FRANCIS BACON

Truth has bounds; error has none.

—WILLIAM BLAKE

Since all is illusion and truth escapes
  us, let us pursue beauty.

—ANATOLE FRANCE

Beauty is truth, truth beauty — that
  is all ye know on earth, and all ye
  need to know.

—JOHN KEATS

Beauty in things exists in the
  mind which contemplates them.

—DAVID HUME

Human love is the desire for union
  with a beautiful object in order to
  make eternity available to mortal life.

—MARSILIO FICINO

Man makes holy what he believes
  as he makes beautiful what he loves.

                    —ERNEST RENAN

What is beautiful is good, and
  who is good will soon be beautiful.

                        —SAPPHO

In the search for beauty and goodness,
  a quest for truth, how easy it is
  to be corrupted.

                    —E. B. WHITE

Where does beauty begin and
  where does it end? Where it ends
  is where the artist begins.

                    —JOHN CAGE

The great artist is the simplifier.

                —HENRI FRÉDÉRIC AMIEL

There is no greatness where simplicity,
  goodness and truth are absent.

                    —TOLSTOY

Simplicity is that grace which
  frees the soul from unnecessary
  reflections upon itself.

                —FRANÇOIS FÉNELON

In character, in manners, in style,
  in all things, the supreme excellence
  is simplicity.

                — LONGFELLOW

Purity and simplicity are the two
  wings with which man soars above
  the earth and all temporary nature.

                —THOMAS À KEMPIS

Unto the pure all things are pure.

                    —TITUS I

Unless the vessel's pure,
all you pour in turns sour.

—HORACE

The highest purpose is
to have no purpose at all.

—JOHN CAGE

Art has its origin in the need to
pretend that human life is something
other than it is, and, in a sense,
by pretending this, it succeeds
to some extent in transforming it.

—EDMUND WILSON

The artist is a dreamer consenting
to dream of the actual world.

—GEORGE SANTAYANA

An artist must know how to convince
others of the truth of his lies.

—PABLO PICASSO

Never reveal anything.

—ROBERT J. FLAHERTY

Be obscure clearly.

—E. B. WHITE

Art is too superior to life
to be satisfied with copying it.

—MARCEL PROUST

Art disenchants; and this
is a great merit. It teaches how
little of what might be, is; how far
beneath our capabilities we ourselves
are content to remain.

—JOHN LANCASTER SPALDING

The real artist's work
is a surprise to himself.

—ROBERT HENRI

Art flourishes where there
is a sense of adventure.

—ALFRED NORTH WHITEHEAD

Art is not a thing; it is a way.

—ELBERT G. HUBBARD

It is art that makes life, makes
interest, makes importance, for
our consideration and application
of these things, and I know of no
substitute whatever for the force
and beauty of its process.

—HENRY JAMES

Art is the demonstration that
the ordinary is extraordinary.

—AMÉDÉE OZENFANT

It is the treating of the commonplace
with the feeling of the sublime
that gives art its true power.

—JEAN F. MILLET

We have art so that we
may not perish by the truth.

—NIETZSCHE

All art constantly aspires
towards the condition of music.

—WALTER PATER

When I hear music I fear no danger.
I am invulnerable. I see no foe.
I am related to the earliest times,
and to the latest.

—THOREAU

It is when the soul has regrets, it
is during the first sorrows of the
autumnal days of life, it is when
one sees mistrust arise like a grim
phantom behind every countryside
hedge, that it is good to have
recourse to music. The fine arts
are made to console.

—STENDHAL

Any work of sculpture
or music that elevates and purifies
your feelings must correspond
to some spiritual reality.

—MARCEL PROUST

After silence, that which
comes nearest to expressing
the inexpressible is music.

—ALDOUS HUXLEY

Music is the only sensual pleasure
without vice.

—SAMUEL JOHNSON

Music is the poetry of the air.

        —JEAN PAUL RICHTER

If poetry comes not as naturally
  as leaves to a tree it had better
  not come at all.

        —JOHN KEATS

Poetry is the spontaneous
  overflow of powerful feelings: it
  takes its origin from emotion
  recollected in tranquillity.

        —WILLIAM WORDSWORTH

Perfect things in poetry do not seem
  strange, they seem inevitable.

        —JORGE LUIS BORGES

Science is for those who learn; poetry
  for those who know.

        —JOSEPH ROUX

Art is I; Science is we.

        —CLAUDE BERNARD

The secret of life is in art.

        —OSCAR WILDE

The genuine productions of art,
  like those of nature, are all
  distinct from each other.

        —JOHN CONSTABLE

When I look at a fig tree, every leaf
  has a different design. They all have
  their own manner of moving in
  space; yet in their own separate ways,
  they all cry, "fig tree."

        —MATISSE

The greatness of man is made up
  of the sole destiny of the species:
  each individual is an empire.

        —ANTOINE DE SAINT-EXUPÉRY

What makes an artist, you see,
  are the moments when he feels
  that he is more than a man.

        —LE CORBUSIER

I feel that art has something to do
  with the achievement of stillness in
  the midst of chaos. A stillness which
  characterizes prayer, too, and the
  eye of the storm. I think art has
  something to do with an arrest of
  attention in the midst of distraction.

        —SAUL BELLOW

Art is not a handicraft, it is a
 transmission of feeling the
 artist has experienced.

—TOLSTOY

Drawing is not what one sees,
 but what others must be made to see.

—DEGAS

Painting isn't an aesthetic operation;
 it's a form of magic designed as a
 mediator between this strange,
 hostile world and us, a way of
 seizing the power by giving form
 to our terrors as well as our desires.

—PABLO PICASSO

Art hath an enemy called ignorance.

—BEN JONSON

Art strives for form
 and hopes for beauty.

—GEORGE BELLOWS

It was at the age of seventy-three
 that I almost understood the form
 and true nature of birds, of fish
 and of plants.

—HOKUSAI

Without freedom, no art; art lives
  only on the restraints it imposes on
  itself, and dies of all others.

                    —ALBERT CAMUS

The more constraints one imposes,
  the more one frees one's self.

                    —IGOR STRAVINSKY

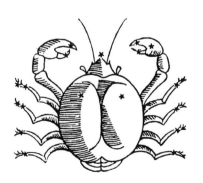

In the studio you learn to conform,
  to submit yourself to the demands
  of your craft so that you may finally
  be free. Your goal is freedom, but
  freedom may only be achieved
  through discipline.

                    —MARTHA GRAHAM

At the last moments like all great acts
  it is pure risk. That is true for me as
  a human being and a writer.

                    —KATHERINE MANSFIELD

Once the risk has really been
  taken, then the greatest danger
  is to risk too much.

                    —KIERKEGAARD

Nothing noble is done without risk.

                    —MONTAIGNE

Danger is a good teacher,
  and makes apt scholars. So are
disgrace, defeat, and exposure
to immediate scorn and laughter.

—WILLIAM HAZLITT

There is only one step from
  the sublime to the ridiculous.

—NAPOLEON I

Embarrassment is to the mind
  what dizziness is to the body.

—LUDWIG BÖRNE

There is no fate that cannot
  be surmounted by scorn.

—ALBERT CAMUS

The courage of self-affirmation
  will not be shaken by the anxiety
  of guilt and condemnation.

—PAUL TILLICH

How sweet it is to remember dangers
  when they are past and gone.

—EURIPIDES

Sweet are the uses of adversity, which
  like the toad, ugly and venomous,
  wears yet a precious jewel in his head.

—SHAKESPEARE

Greater dooms win greater destinies.

—HERACLITUS

Every calamity is a spur
  and valuable hint.

—EMERSON

Adversity reveals genius,
  prosperity conceals it.

—HORACE

Adversity is the first path to truth.

—LORD BYRON

Art does not reproduce the visible;
rather, it makes visible

—PAUL KLEE

Art is but a point of view and genius
but a way of looking at things.

—HENRY JAMES

Genius is the capacity for seeing
relationships where lesser men
see none.

—WILLIAM JAMES

Genius is only a superior
power of seeing.

—JOHN RUSKIN

I do believe that works of genius
are the first things in this world.

—JOHN KEATS

Genius is eternal patience.

—MICHELANGELO

Genius begins great works;
labor alone finishes them.

—JOSEPH JOUBERT

I know of no such thing as genius;
it is nothing but labor and diligence.

—WILLIAM HOGARTH

All works of genius persuade us that
they were effortless of achievement.

—VITA SACKVILLE-WEST

Genius always remains
most inexplicable to itself.

—SCHILLER

To do what others cannot do is talent,
to do what talent cannot do is genius.

—WILL HENRY

Talent is what you possess;
genius is what possesses you.

—MALCOLM COWLEY

Genius does what it must,
and talent does what it can.

—OWEN MEREDITH

All of us are born with genius,
but most people only keep it
for a few seconds.

—EDGARD VARESE

In relation to genius the public
is a clock that runs slow.

—CHARLES BAUDELAIRE

Mediocrity knows nothing
  higher than itself, but talent
  instantly recognizes genius.

—SIR ARTHUR CONAN DOYLE

Great spirits have always
  encountered violent opposition
  from mediocre minds.

—ALBERT EINSTEIN

Mediocre people have an
  answer to everything and are
  astonished at nothing.

—EUGÈNE DELACROIX

It is a great sign of mediocrity
  always to praise moderately.

—VAUVENARGUES

When you praise someone
  you call yourself his equal.

—GOETHE

Whatever is in any way beautiful
  hath its source of beauty in itself;
  praise forms no part of it. So it
  is none the worse nor the better
  for being praised.

—MARCUS AURELIUS

You do ill if you praise, but
  worse if you censure, what
  you do not rightly understand.

—LEONARDO DA VINCI

The true genius is a mind of large
general powers, accidently determined to some particular direction.

—SAMUEL JOHNSON

It is the essence of genius
to make use of the simplest idea.

—CHARLES PÉGUY

It takes a kind of genius to make
a fortune, and especially a large
fortune. It is neither goodness,
nor wit, nor talent, nor strength,
nor delicacy. I don't know
precisely what it is: I am waiting
for someone to tell me.

—JEAN DE LA BRUYÈRE

To be clever enough to get
a great deal of money, one must
be stupid enough to want it.

—G. K. CHESTERTON

There is no sin except stupidity.

—OSCAR WILDE

Intelligent people make many blunders
because they never believe the world
to be as stupid as it is.

—NICOLAS CHAMFORT

The fundamental cause of trouble
in the world today is that the stupid
are cocksure and the intelligent
are full of doubt.

—BERTRAND RUSSELL

Neither a lofty degree of intelligence
nor imagination nor both together
go to the making of genius. Love,
love, love, that is the soul of genius.

—MOZART

Very simple ideas lie within the reach
only of complex minds.

—RÉMY DE GOURMONT

Winter

JANUARY

For now we see through a glass, darkly;
But then face to face: now I know in part;
But then shall I know even as also
I am known.

—THE BIBLE, I Corinthians

ANUARY is named for Janus, an ancient Roman deity and spiritual guardian of gates and doorways. Like a door, Janus was portrayed as having two opposite faces: one looked to the past while the other faced the future. As the god who presided over all beginnings, it is clear why Romans readily accepted January to replace March as the first month of the year in the reformed Julian calendar.

In fifteenth-century rural France, however, the new year still began in springtime. The dead of winter was a quiet reflective time to enjoy the warmth of the hearth and ruminate on life's mystery. Attended by a faithful companion, our medieval gentleman sups alone in comfort — a roaring fire warming his back, a cushion shielding his feet from the cold floor tiles.

When this woodcut was made, Saturn was considered the astrological ruler of Capricorn and Aquarius. The most remote planet suited the winter season as did the god's theme of limitation. Paradoxically, happiness and contentment typified his reign: the mythical Age of Saturn, Sower of Seed. The artist depicts a winged Aquarius pouring water from two urns rather than the usual one. A visual bid for goodness and rain?

Spiritual awareness is said to be keenest when the landscape is bleak and life retreats indoors.

There is no such thing as chance;
and what seems to us the
merest accident springs from
the deepest source of destiny.

—SCHILLER

Like puppets we are
moved by outside strings.

—HORACE

Everything is determined, the
beginning as well as the end, by
forces over which we have no
control. It is determined for the
insect as well as for the star.
Human beings, vegetables, or
cosmic dust, we all dance to a
mysterious tune, intoned in
the distance by an invisible piper.

—ALBERT EINSTEIN

Only for his dreams is a man
responsible — his actions are
what he must do. Actions are a
bastard race to which a man has
not given his full paternity.

—WILLIAM BUTLER YEATS

How often the activity of our life
is the least real part of it.

—JOSEPH CONRAD

The basis of action is lack of
imagination. It is the last resource of
those who know not how to dream.

—OSCAR WILDE

Toil, feel, think, hope; you will
be sure to dream enough before
you die without arranging for it.

—JOHN STERLING

Dreams are true while they last,
and do we not live in dreams?

—ALFRED, LORD TENNYSON

The older I become, the more
I realize that dreams are
something which do not fade.

—JEAN COCTEAU

In dreams begins resdponsibillity.

—WILLIAM BUTLER YEATS

Hope is a waking dream.

—ARISTOTLE

The natural flights of the human
mind are not from pleasure
to pleasure, but from hope to hope.

—SAMUEL JOHNSON

Hope is the last gift given to man,
and the only gift not given to youth.
The power of hoping through
everything, the knowledge that
the soul survives its adventures,
that great inspiration comes
to the middle-aged.

—G. K. CHESTERTON

We don't need to continue living
the way we lived yesterday. Free
yourself of that idea and a thousand
possibilities beckon to a new life.

—CHRISTIAN MORGENSTERN

Man cannot discover new oceans
unless he has courage to lose sight
of the shore.

—ANDRÉ GIDE

The larger the island of knowledge,
the longer the shoreline of wonder.

—RALPH W. SOCKMAN

As knowledge increases,
wonder deepens.

—CHARLES MORGAN

Wonder rather than doubt
is the root of knowledge.

—ABRAHAM JOSHUA HESCHEL

The first step to knowledge
is to know that we are ignorant.

—ROBERT CECIL

What we know here is very little, but
what we are ignorant of is immense.

—PIERRE SIMON LAPLACE

One part of knowledge consists
in being ignorant of such things
as are not worth knowing.

—CRATES

A person is never happy except
at the price of some ignorance.

—ANATOLE FRANCE

The price of knowledge
is loss of the innocence of life.

—LUDWIG FEUERBACH

It is not only our fate but
our business to lose innocence,
and once we have lost that, it is
futile to attempt a picnic in Eden.

—ELIZABETH BOWEN

Ignorance is a prolonged infancy,
only deprived of its charm.

—MARQUIS DE BOUFFLERS

By ignorance is pride increased;
Those most assume who know least.

—JOHN GAY

The best lack all conviction while the
worst are full of passionate intensity.

—ALDOUS HUXLEY

When they asked Plato how he had
lived in this world he answered:
"I entered with pain. I never ceased
to marvel. I depart with reluctance.
And I have learned nothing except
that I know nothing."

—GOETHE

None are wise by natural instinct.

—ARISTOTLE

Addiction to knowledge is like
any other addiction; it offers an
escape from the fear of emptiness,
of loneliness, of frustration, the
fear of being nothing.

— KRISHNAMURTI

Study has been my sovereign remedy
against life's disappointments. I
have never known any distress that
an hour's reading did not relieve.

—MONTESQUIEU

A scholar has no ennui.

—JEAN PAUL RICHTER

Truly wise you are not unless your
wisdom be constantly changing from
your childhood on to your death.

—MAURICE MAETERLINCK

The only means of strengthening one's
intellect is to make up one's mind
about nothing — to let the mind
be a thoroughfare for all thoughts.

—JOHN KEATS

It is only when we forget all our
learning that we begin to know.

—THOREAU

Knowledge cuts up the world;
wisdom makes it whole.

—DAVID MAYBURY-LEWIS

To repent nothing is
the beginning of wisdom.

—LUDWIG BÖRNE

He dares to be a fool, and that is the
first step in the direction of wisdom.

—JAMES GIBBONS HUNEKER

If a fool would persist in his folly,
he would become wise.

—WILLIAM BLAKE

Luck, mere luck, may make
even madness wisdom.

—DOUGLAS JERROLD

It is characteristic of wisdom
not to do desperate things.

—THOREAU

Common sense in an
uncommon degree is what
the world calls wisdom.

—COLERIDGE

Common sense is not so common.

—VOLTAIRE

Common sense is the measure
of the possible.

—HENRI FRÉDÉRIC AMIEL

What grace is to the body
good sense is to the mind.

—LA ROCHEFOUCAULD

The mind in each one of us is a god.

—EURIPIDES

God is but a word invoked
to explain the world.

—LAMARTINE

The nature of god is a circle
of which the center is everywhere
and the circumference is no where.

—EMPEDOCLES

We know God easily if we
do not constrain to define him.

—JOSEPH JOUBERT

It is Socrates' opinion, and mine too,
that the wisest theory about the gods
is to have no theory at all.

—MONTAIGNE

Our humanity were a poor thing
were it not for the divinity
which stirs within us.

—SIR FRANCIS BACON

There's a divinity that shapes our ends,
rough-hew them how we will.

—SHAKESPEARE

I believe in Spinoza's God who
reveals himself in the orderly
harmony of what exists, not in a
God who concerns himself with
fates and actions of human beings.

—RABINDRANATH TAGORE

Religion is human experience
interpreted by human imagination.

—GEORGE SANTAYANA

There is nothing that fear or hope
does not make men believe.

—VAUVENARGUES

As to the gods, I have no means
of knowing either that they exist or
that they do not exist. For many are
the obstacles that impede knowledge,
both the obscurity of the question
and the shortness of human life.

—PROTAGORAS

Men have feverishly conceived
a heaven only to find it insipid,
and a hell to find it ridiculous.

—GEORGE SANTAYANA

Who has not found the Heaven
below, will fail of it above.

—EMILY DICKINSON

What you cannot find on earth
is not worth seeking.

—NORMAN DOUGLAS

It is one of the beautiful
compensations of this life that
no one can sincerely try to help
another without helping himself.

—CHARLES DUDLEY WARNER

Virtue is an affair of deeds and does
not need a store of words or learning.

—ANTISTHENES

He who wishes to secure the good
of others, has already secured
his own.

—CONFUCIUS

The luxury of doing good surpasses
every other personal enjoyment.

—JOHN GAY

An effort made for the happiness of
others lifts us above ourselves.

—LYDIA MARIA CHILD

Happiness is the only sanction
of life; where happiness fails,
existence remains a mad and
lamentable experiment.

—GEORGE SANTAYANA

Whether happiness may come
or not, we should try and prepare
one's self to do without it.

—GEORGE ELIOT

I think human beings are
fundamentally crushed by
a sense of their insignificance.

—VIRGINIA WOOLF

Every man takes the limit
of his own field of vision
for the limits of the world.

—SCHOPENHAUER

There are many religions,
but there is only one morality.

—JOHN RUSKIN

If you look at life one way,
there is always cause for alarm.

—ELIZABETH BOWEN

Everything is a dangerous drug
except reality, which is unendurable.

—CYRIL CONNOLLY

Every form of addiction is bad,
no matter whether the narcotic be
alcohol or morphine or idealism.

—CARL G. JUNG

Idealism increases in direct proportion
to one's distance from the problem.

—JOHN GALSWORTHY

Reality doesn't always come up to
the ideal, you know. But that doesn't
make me believe any less in the ideal.

—ALDOUS HUXLEY

I am an idealist. I don't know
where I'm going but I'm on my way.

—CARL SANDBURG

There is nothing in reality
that conforms strictly to logic.

—NIETZSCHE

One cannot help but be in awe
when one contemplates the mysteries
of eternity, of life, of the marvelous
structure of reality. It is enough if
one tries merely to comprehend
a little of this mystery each day.

—ALBERT EINSTEIN

Ultimate reality cannot be understood
except intuitively, through an act
of will and the affections.

—ALDOUS HUXLEY

Go into yourself and see how deep the
place is from which your life flows.

—RILKE

I believe when you give yourself up
to complete and utter concentration,
the brain will give you information
that doesn't come from reason.

—BENJAMIN BRYAN

The mind can proceed only so far
upon what it knows and can prove.
There comes a point where the mind
takes a higher plane of knowledge,
but can never prove how it got there.
All great discoveries have involved
such a leap.

—ALBERT EINSTEIN

A moment's insight is sometimes
worth a life's experience.

—OLIVER WENDELL HOLMES

The world lives and breathes,
and we can draw its spirit into us.

—MASILIO FICINO

As far as we can discern, the sole
 purpose of human existence
is to kindle a light in the darkness
of being.

—CARL G. JUNG

Man is not born to solve the
 problems of the universe, but to
find out what he has to do; and
to restrain himself within the limits
of his comprehension.

—GOETHE

Your mistake lies in believing that
 man was put on this earth to do
something.

—EDMUND ABOUT

If you do not expect it,
 you will not find the unexpected,
for it is hard to find and difficult,

—HERACLITUS

A serious study of any important
 body of knowledge, or theory, or
belief, if undertaken with a critical
but not a cruel mind, will in the end
yield some secret, some valuable
permanent insight, into the nature
of life and the true end of man.

—ROBERTSON DAVIES

It is good to love the unknown.

—CHARLES LAMB

Heaven sends down its good
 and evil symbols and wise men
act accordingly.

—CONFUCIUS

Stones are silent teachers;
 they force silence on the observer,
and the best that one learns from
them cannot be communicated.

—GOETHE

Sometimes a tree tells you more
 than can be read in books.

—CARL G. JUNG

The soul without imagination
is what an observatory would
be without a telescope.

—HENRY WARD BEECHER

We do not see the lens
through which we look.

—RUTH BENEDICT

Of soul thou shalt never find
boundaries, not if thou trackest
it on every path; so deep is its cause.

—HERACLITUS

God may or may not exist. But there is
the empirical fact that contemplation
of the divinity — of goodness in its
most unqualified form — is a method
of realizing that goodness in some
slight degree is in one's own life.

—ALDOUS HUXLEY

Mystery is the only life of the soul.

—CÉLINE

Call the world if you please
The Vale of Soul-making.

—JOHN KEATS

Nowhere can a man find a quieter
or more untroubled retreat
than in his own soul.

—MARCUS AURELIUS

Your soul is a choice landscape.

—PAUL VERLAINE

The soul is strong
that trusts in goodness.

—PHILIP MASSINGER

Everyone should know that
you can't live in any other way
than by cultivating the soul.

—APULEIUS

It is never too early or too late
to care for the well-being of the soul.

—EPICURUS

Conscience is the voice of the soul.

—JEAN JACQUES ROUSSEAU

Sin is whatever obscures the soul.

—ANDRÉ GIDE

The soul is partly in eternity
and partly in time.

—MARSILIO FICINO

Oh my soul, do not aspire
to immortal life, but exhaust
the limits of the possible.

—PINDAR

The soul deserves to be immortal.

—VIRGINIA WOOLF

I have said that the soul is not
more than the body, and I have
said that the body is not more than
the soul, and nothing, not God,
is greater to one than one's self.

—WALT WHITMAN

For me the conviction of the
continuing existence derives from the
concept of activity: for if I continue to
be unremittingly active until my end,
nature will be obliged to assign
to me another form of existence
when the present one is no longer
able to endure my spirit.

—GOETHE

I have been, ere now, a boy and a girl,
a bush, a bird, a dumb fish in the sea.

—EMPEDOCLES

I am too much of a skeptic
to deny the possibility of anything.

—THOMAS HENRY HUXLEY

Virtue is the essential preliminary
to the mystical experience.

—ALDOUS HUXLEY

All earthly desires are sweeter
in expectation than in enjoyment;
but all spiritual pleasures more
in fruition than expectation.

—OWEN FELTHAM

It was previously a question of
finding out whether or not life
had to have a meaning to be lived.
It now becomes clear, on the
contrary, that it will be lived all the
better if it has no meaning.

—ALBERT CAMUS

The meaningless absurdity of life
is the only incontestable knowledge
accessible to man.

—TOLSTOY

Taken as a whole,
the universe is absurd.

—WALTER SAVAGE LANDOR

The man who has no inner life
is a slave of his surroundings.

      —HENRI FRÉDÉRIC AMIEL

Solitude is to the mind what
fasting is to the body, fatal if it
is too prolonged, and yet necessary.

      —VAUVENARGUES

Solitude makes us tougher
toward ourselves and tenderer
toward others: in both ways it
improves our character.

      —NIETZSCHE

The more I find myself
by myself and alone, the
more I become a lover of myth.

      —ARISTOTLE

Myth has four layers
of meaning: literal, moral,
allegorical, and metaphysical.

      —BOCCACCIO

A man's life of any worth is
a continual allegory, and very few
eyes can see the mystery of his life.

      —JOHN KEATS

Mythology teaches you what's
behind the literature and the arts,
it teaches you about your own life.

      —JOSEPH CAMPBELL

Deeper meaning resides in the fairy
tales told to me in childhood than
in the truth that is taught by life.

      —SCHILLER

What flows into you from
the myth is not truth but reality
(truth is always about something
but reality is about which truth is)
and therefore every myth becomes
the father of innumerable truths
on the abstract level.

      —C. S. LEWIS

It has taken us two thousand
years to get around again
to meditating on mythology.

      —EZRA POUND

Winter

FEBRUARY

*We shall not cease from exploration
And the end of all our exploring
Will be to arrive where we started
And know the place for the first time.*

—T. S. ELIOT

THE Latin word *februa* means "to purify by sacrifice" and as the month's primary festival in Roman times was the Lupercalia, from *lupus*, wolf, we may conjecture that February describes this, the oldest Roman holiday. Born with the city's earliest settlements, the rite of the circuit around the Palantine Hill in late winter may have been originally intended to drive off wolves or as another theory suggests, on this site the legendary Romulus and Remus were nurtured by a she-wolf. Faunus, the Roman Pan, was called Lupercus, he who protects flocks from attacks by wolves, and was honored at the Lupercalia. Imperial Rome saw the annual ceremony conducted by priests drawn from patrician families circle the hill striking all women in their path with whips made from the skin of a sacrificed goat. A blow received was believed to drive out the demon of barrenness.

February finds our Lord of the Manor on his feet demanding more wood to fuel his hearth fire. Outdoor activity commences as the sign of Aquarius is succeeded by Jupiter's Fish. The artist's own invention, the third fish, has borne issue and now five fish represent Pisces in the zodiacal inset, an optimistic symbol of fecundity.

The distinguished panel of fellow travelers prepare our minds, hearts and souls for another cycle of seasons.

Nothing is given so freely as advice.

—LA ROCHEFOUCAULD

Advice is seldom welcome;
  and those who want it the most
  always like it the least.

—LORD CHESTERFIELD

There is nothing which we receive
  with so much reluctance as advice.

—JOSEPH ADDISON

Many receive advice,
  only the wise profit by it.

—PUBLILIUS SYRUS

Whatever your advice, make it brief.

—HORACE

When anger spreads through
  the breast, guard thy tongue
  from barking idly.

—SAPPHO

Laughter cannot bring back
  what anger has driven away.

—JAPANESE PROVERB

There is, however, a limit at which
  forebearance ceases to be a virtue.

—EDMUND BURKE

The world often continues to allow
  evil because it isn't angry enough.

—BEDE JARRETT

Usually when people are sad, they
  don't do anything. They just cry
  over their condition. But when they
  get angry, they bring about change.

—MALCOLM X

He who accepts evil without
  protesting against it
  is really cooperating with it.

—MARTIN LUTHER KING, JR.

There are two things to which
  we must resign ourselves on pain of
  finding life unbearable; the ravages
  of time and human injustice.

—NICOLAS CHAMFORT

Treading on others
  adds nothing to our stature.

—ELLEN GLASGOW

It is human nature to hate the man
  whom you have hurt.

—TACITUS

Never find your delight
  in another's misfortune.

—PUBLILIUS SYRUS

We grow tired of everything
  but turning others into ridicule,
  and congratulating ourselves
  on their defects.

—WILLIAM HAZLITT

Do not sit among the mockers,
  they are the meanest of creatures.

—MATTHIAS CLAUDIUS

It is a malady confined to man,
  and not seen in any other creatures,
  to hate and despise ourselves.

—MONTAIGNE

Perhaps the only true dignity of man
  is his capacity to despise himself.

—GEORGE SANTAYANA

Irony is the last phase of disillusion.

—ANATOLE FRANCE

The one guardian of life is love,
  but to be loved you must love.

—MARSILIO FICINO

The human heart, at whatever
  age, opens only to the heart
  that opens in return.

—MARIA EDGEWORTH

A loving heart is the truest wisdom.

—CHARLES DICKENS

She that is loved is safe, and he
  that loves is joyful. Love is a union
  of all things excellant.

—JEREMY TAYLOR

There's nothing worth the wear
  of winning, but laughter
  and the love of friends.

—HILAIRE BELLOC

Serious things cannot be understood
without laughable things, nor
opposites at all without opposites.

—PLATO

Man is the only animal that laughs
and weeps; for he is the only animal
that is struck by the difference
between what things are
and what they might have been.

—WILLIAM HAZLITT

The young man who has not wept
is a savage, and the old man
who will not laugh is a fool.

—GEORGE SANTAYANA

Too much gravity
argues a shallow mind.

—JOHANN KASPAR LAVATER

We should take everything seriously
but nothing tragically.

—ADOLPHE THIERS

It is almost as important to know what
is not serious as to know what is.

—JOHN KENNETH GALBRAITH

It is a curious fact that people
are never so trivial as when
they take themselves seriously.

—OSCAR WILDE

The most perfect humour and irony
is generally quite unconscious.

—SAMUEL BUTLER

Some men have acted courage who
had it not; but no man can act wit.

—LORD HALIFAX

If you want to be witty,
work on your character and say
what you think on every occasion.

—STENDHAL

If you want to make people weep,
you must weep yourself. If you
want to make people laugh, your
face must remain serious.

—CASANOVA

There is no possibility of being witty
without a little ill-nature.

—RICHARD BRINSLEY SHERIDAN

Satire should, like a polished razor
keen, wound with a touch
that's scarcely felt or seen.

—LADY MARY WORTLEY MONTAGU

Wit is the clash and reconcilement
of incongruities, the meeting of
extremes round a corner.

—LEIGH HUNT

Life is a series of relapses
and recoveries.

—GEORGE ADE

There are moments when everything
turns out right. Don't let it alarm
you: they pass.

—JULES RENARD

Whatsoever there is in the world
is waxing or waning.

—FERNANDO DE ROJAS

If all men would bring their
misfortunes together in one place,
most would be glad to take his
own troubles home again, rather
than to take a proportion
out of the common stock.

—SOLON

The human heart has a tiresome
tendency to label as fate only what
crushes it. But happiness, likewise,
in its way, is without reason,
since it is inevitable.

—ALBERT CAMUS

I must confess I should not know
what to do with eternal bliss, if it
did not present me with new problems
and difficulties to overcome.

—GOETHE

A lifetime of happiness!
No man alive could bear it;
it would be hell on earth.

—GEORGE BERNARD SHAW

It is in changing that things find repose.

—HERACLITUS

Heaven from all creatures
hides the book of fate.

—ALEXANDER POPE

Fate sells what we think she gives.

—MONTENEGRIN PROVERB

Necessity never made a good bargain.

—BENJAMIN FRANKLIN

A bargain is in its very essence
a hostile transaction.

—LORD BYRON

Those who do not see themselves
as victims accept the greater stress.

—SHIRLEY HAZZARD

Humanity is composed but of two
catagories, the invalids and the nurses.

—WALTER SICKERT

The worst form of tyranny the
world has ever known: the tyranny
of the weak over the strong.
It is the only tyranny that lasts.

—OSCAR WILDE

Those who do not feel pain
seldom think that it is felt.

—SAMUEL JOHNSON

No one ever feels helpless by the
side of the self-helper; whilst the
self-sacrificer is always a drag, a
responsibility, a reproach, an everlast-
ing and unnatural trouble with
whom no really strong soul can live.

—GEORGE BERNARD SHAW

No man is weak from choice.

—VAUVENARGUES

Few things are harder to put up with
than a good example.

—MARK TWAIN

From a worldly point of view,
there is no mistake so great
as that of always being right.

—SAMUEL BUTLER

It is better to ask some of the questions
than to know all the answers.

—JAMES THURBER

Do not wish to be anything but what
you are, and try to be that perfectly.

—ST. FRANCIS DE SALES

For all your ills I give you laughter.

—RABELAIS

As we are now living in an eternity
the time to be happy is today.

—GLENVILLE KLEISER

To be happy you must have
taken the measure of your powers,
tasted the fruits of your passion,
and learned your place in the world.

—GEORGE SANTAYANA

Though the most be players,
some must be spectators.

—BEN JONSON

Learning to live is learning to let go.

—SOGYAL RINPOCHE

You must let yourself go along in life
like a cork in the current of a stream.

—AUGUSTE RENOIR

Tomorrow's tangle to the winds resign.

—OMAR KHAYYAM

Nothing fixes a thing so intensely in
the memory as the wish to forget it.

—MONTAIGNE

Memory is a crazy woman that hoards
colored rags and throws away food.

—AUSTIN O'MALLEY

Vanity plays lurid tricks
with our memory.

—JOSEPH CONRAD

The eyes of memory see nothing
if we strain them too hard.

—MARCEL PROUST

Intuition picks up
the key that memory drops.

—EMILY DICKINSON

Unless we remember
we cannot understand.

—E. M. FORSTER

Memory is life's clock.

—JUAN GRAJALES

The present is never our object; the past and the present we use as a means; the future only is our end.

—BLAISE PASCAL

Real generosity toward the future consists in giving all to what is present.

—ALBERT CAMUS

The present joys of life we doubly taste by looking back with pleasure to the past.

—MARTIAL

Think only of the past as its remembrance gives you pleasure.

—JANE AUSTEN

The test of pleasure is the memory that it leaves behind.

—JEAN PAUL RICHTER

All that is worth remembering of life is the poetry of it.

—WILLIAM HAZLITT

Everything in the past died yesterday; everything in the future was born today.

—CHINESE PROVERB

Today means boundless and inexhaustible eternity. Months and years and all periods of time are concepts of men, who gauge everything by number, but the true name of eternity is Today.

—PHILO

What shall be tomorrow, think not of asking. Each day that fortune gives you, be it what it may, set down for gain.

—HORACE

We are tomorrow's past.

—MARY WEBB

Only the past is immortal.

—DELMORE SCHWARTZ

Hope springs eternal
in the human breast.

—ALEXANDER POPE

Hope is life and life is hope.

—ADELE SHREVE

We hope vaguely but dread precisely.

—PAUL VALÉRY

The miserable have no other medicine
but only hope.

—SHAKESPEARE

Patience is the art of hoping.

—VAUVENARGUES

Faith is not the beginning
but the end of all knowledge.

—GOETHE

Faith must trample underfoot
all reason, sense and understanding.

—MARTIN LUTHER

I had to set limits to knowledge
in order to make place for faith.

—IMMANUEL KANT

A faith that cannot survive
collision with the truth
is not worth many regrets.

—ARTHUR C. CLARKE

Faith has need of the whole truth.

—PIERRE TEILHARD DE CHARDIN

The ideal is but truth
glimpsed from afar.

—LAMARTINE

The faith waiting in the heart
  of a seed promises a miracle of life
  which it cannot prove.

—RABINDRANATH TAGORE

Faith and love have one thing
  in common: neither of them
  can be created by compulsion.

—SCHOPENHAUER

A sudden impulse that
  cannot be defined at times
  takes hold of us and makes us love.

—CORNEILLE

There is nothing in love
  but what we imagine.

—SAINTE-BEUVE

Love is a reality in the
  domain of the imagination.

—TALLEYRAND

Love is the triumph of
  imagination over intelligence.

—H. L. MENCKEN

Love, it has been said, does not
  obey the rules of love but yields
  to some more ancient and ruder law.

—MARTHA GRAHAM

You can never do a kindness
  too soon, for you never know
  how soon it will be too late.

—EMERSON

There never was a person that did
  anything worth doing, who did not
  really receive more than he gave.

—HENRY WARD BEECHER

The more he gives to others,
  the more he has for his own.

—LAO-TSE

Slow in giving is next to refusing.

—FRENCH PROVERB

Men do less than they ought,
  unless they do all that they can.

—THOMAS CARLYLE

In charity there is no excess.

—SIR FRANCIS BACON

This only is charity,
  to do all, all that we can.

—JOHN DONNE

Virtue is bold, and
  goodness never fearful.

—SHAKESPEARE

So act that your principle of action
  might safely be made a law
for the whole world.

—IMMANUEL KANT

Integrity has no need of rules.

—ALBERT CAMUS

Life is very short, and uncertain;
  let us spend it as well as we can.

—SAMUEL JOHNSON

Chaos is the law of nature,
  order is the dream of man.

—HENRY ADAMS

When the best things
  are not possible, the best
may be made of those that are.

—RICHARD HOOKER

Every day that dawns is a gift to me and
  I take it that way. I accept it
gratefully without looking beyond it.

—MATISSE

Wisdom comes by disillusionment.

—GEORGE SANTAYANA

A small debt produces a debtor;
  a heavy one an enemy.

—PUBLILIUS SYRUS

It is the enemy whom we do not
  suspect who is the most dangerous.

—FERNANDO DE ROJAS

O wise man, wash your hands
  of that friend who associates
  with your enemy.

—SAADI

A needle's eye is wide enough
  for two friends; the whole world
is too narrow for two enemies.

—PERSIAN PROVERB

Speak well of your friend,
  of your enemy say nothing.

—ENGLISH PROVERB

A good word is an easy obligation;
  but not to speak ill, requires only
  our silence which costs us nothing.

—JOHN TILLOTSON

The subjection of the tongue
  is the most difficult of all victories.

—PYTHAGORAS

Men govern nothing with more
  difficulty than their tongues,
  and can moderate their desires
  more than their words.

—SPINOZA

Time destroys the groundless conceits
of man, but confirms that which
is founded on nature and reality.

—CICERO

Time will explain it all.
He is a talker, and needs no
questioning before he speaks.

—EURIPIDES

Time is a great teacher, but
unfortunately it kills all its pupils.

—HECTOR BERLIOZ

Time is a sort of river of passing events,
and strong is its current; no sooner
is a thing brought to sight than it
is swept by and another takes its place,
and this too will be swept away.

—MARCUS AURELIUS

All is change,
all yields its place and goes.

—EURIPIDES

People themselves alter so much
that there is something new
to be observed in them forever.

—JANE AUSTEN

Everything passes, everything breaks,
everything wearies.

—FRENCH PROVERB

Giving up is the ultimate tragedy.

—ROBERT J. DONOVAN

Life is not giving up, but moving on.

—MARTHA GRAHAM

Our greatest glory is not
in never falling but in rising
every time we fall.

—CONFUCIUS

Life is a language in which
certain truths are conveyed to us;
if we could learn them in some
other way, we should not live.

—SCHOPENHAUER

Dreams, as well as reason,
often change with each new season.

—ENGLISH PROVERB

The only joy in the world is to begin.

—CESARE PAVESE

Push on, and faith
will catch up with you.

—JEAN LE ROND D'ALEMBERT

INDEX

novelist. 86

Scott, Winfield Townley (1910-1968), American poet. 22

Seattle, Chief (1786-1866), American Indian tribal leader (Seatlh). 117, 127

Seneca, Lucius Annaeus (4 BC-AD 65), Roman philosopher. 9, 13, 26, 29, 30, 31, 44, 54, 55, 74, 85, 88, 89, 92, 101, 102, 103, 107, 134, 140

Sévigné, Mme. Marie de (1626-1696), French letter-writer. 11

Shakespeare, William (1564-1616), English poet, dramatist. 22, 23, 27, 29, 31, 37, 39, 44, 47, 61, 79, 87, 89, 91, 94, 95, 134, 142, 158, 171, 190, 191

Shaw, George Bernard (1856-1950), Anglo-Irish dramatist. 7, 42, 53, 56, 77, 79, 89, 105, 124, 126, 138, 143, 186, 187

Shelley, Percy Bysshe (1792-1822), English poet. 38, 62, 143, 145

Shenstone, William (1714-1763), English poet. 43, 94, 141

Sheridan, Richard Brinsley (1751-1816), English dramatist. 24, 93, 185

Shreve, Adele (1904-), English playwright. 190

Shuttleworth, Philip Nicolas (1782-1842), English prelate. 139

Sickert, Walter (1860-1942), English painter. 187

Sidney, Sir Philip (1554-1586), English poet. 71, 123

Smith, Alexander (1830-1867), Scottish poet. 101

Smith, Logan Pearsall (1865-1946), Anglo-American author. 61, 73

Smith, Roy L., *no data*, 119

Smith, Sydney (1771-1845), English divine. 142

Snow, C. P. (1905-1980), English novelist, scientist. 46

Sockman, Ralph W. (1889-1970), American clergyman. 168

Socrates (469-399 BC), Greek philosopher. 12, 25, 106

Solon (638-559 BC), Greek sage. 124, 186

Sophocles (495-406 BC), Greek poet. 25, 26, 55, 80, 149

Spalding, John Lancaster (1840-1916), American bishop, author. 153

Spinoza, Baruch de (1632-1677), Dutch philosopher. 69, 73, 192

Staël, Mme. de (1766-1817), French author. 40

Stanislas, Leszinski (1677-1766), King of Poland. 71

Steffens, Lincoln (1866-1936), American author. 79

Stein, Gertrude (1874-1946), American writer. 139

Steinbeck, John (1902-1968), American novelist. 28

Stendhal (Henri Beyle) (1783-1842), French novelist. 8, 10, 39, 87, 154, 185

Sterling, John (1806-1844), British author. 167

Sterne, Laurence (1713-1768), English novelist. 60

Stevenson, Robert Louis (1850-1894), British author. 21, 45, 47, 53

Stoddard, Elizabeth (1823-1902), American writer. 40

Stoppard, Tom (1937-), British playwright. 133

Stravinsky, Igor (1882-1971), Russian-born composer. 157

Surtees, R. S. (1803-1864), English writer. 87, 127

Swedenborg, Emanuel (1688-1772), Swedish theologian. 38

Swift, Jonathan (1667-1745), Irish satirist. 85, 106, 108

Tacitus, Cornelius (56-120), Roman historian. 102, 184

Tagore, Rabindranath (1861-1941), Bengali writer. 171, 191

Talleyrand, Charles Maurice de (Perigord) (1754-1838), French politician, diplomat. 191

Tasso, Torquato (1544-1595), Italian poet. 24

Taylor, Jeremy (1613-1667), English divine, author. 123, 184

Taylor, Sir Henry (1800-1886), English poet, dramatist. 138

Teilhard, Pierre de Chardin (1881-1955),

PROVERBS

BOOKS